"That s✱it will never sell!"

Mike,

Thank you so much
for all your brilliant
help.

Best,

David

"That s

never

The real story behind
Baileys Irish Cream
and other great
drinks brands

David Gluckman

*it will sell!"

A book about ideas by
the person who had them

PRIDEAUX PRESS

First published 2017 by Prideaux Press

ISBN: 978-1-5272-0058-6

Text © David Gluckman 2017

Cover design by Jamie Keenan
Page art direction and design
by Simon Daley at Giraffe Books
Copy-editing by Salima Hirani at Giraffe Books
Production by Angela Young

Printed in China

Picture credits

The publishers have made every effort to obtain
the necessary permissions. Please advise of any
omissions or errors and we will rectify these in
subsequent reprints of this book.

14 Shutterstock/Patryk Kosmider; **18–19** Creative
Commons/Jerzy Strzelecki; **21** Creative Commons/
High Contrast; **31** Bob Wagner; **32** Creative
Commons/Ewan Munro; **36** Shutterstock/Slaven;
41 Ornu SCo-operate Limited; **43** Shutterstock/
Azure1; **46–47** Creative Commons/H. Grobe;
53 Master of Malt; **57** Ian Garlick; **60** Shutterstock/
Silberkorn; **68–69** Shutterstock/Lukasz Szwaj;
73 Ian Garlick; **74**, **75** Advertising Archive;
79 AC Cooper; **80** Shutterstock/Brian Mueller;
83 AC Cooper; **84** Gordon Smith; **88** Shutterstock/
Sergey Peterman; **92–93** Creative Commons/Klaus
D Peter; **101** brandnewretro.ie; **105** Shutterstock/
marykatherinedonovan; **109** Ian Garlick;
116 Shutterstock/ Soloviova Liudmyla; **121** AC
Cooper; **125** Ian Garlick; **128–129** Darrell Ireland;
133 AC Cooper; **134–135** Howard Waller; **137** AC
Cooper; **140** Darrell Ireland;**144** Shutterstock/
stockcreations; **147** Ian Garlick; **151** Ian Garlick;
152 Gordon Smith/Shutterstock/somchaij; **157** AC
Cooper; **161** Graham Kirk; **162–163** Shutterstock/
JoffreyM; **167** Ian Garlick; **173** AC Cooper;
176,**177** AC Cooper; **178–179** Shutterstock/Elena
Ermakova; **184** AC Cooper; **187** Ian Garlick;
189 Shutterstock/ Anna Jedynak; **191** AC Cooper;
195 Ian Garlick; **196–197** Shutterstock/ Michael
Leslie; **203** Graham Kirk; **209** AC Cooper; **215** AC
Cooper; **220** Shutterstock/ Peshkova; **223** Bob
Wagner/Ian Garlick; **225** The Whisky Exchange;
226 Ian Garlick; **232** AC Cooper; **235** AC Cooper;
236–237 Public Domain; **238** Ian Garlick; **241** Ian
Garlick/Shutterstock/upixa; **243** Ian Garlick;
245 Scanned by Simon; **247** Shutterstock/drserg;
248 Ian Garlick; **252** AC Cooper; **255** Gordon Smith/
Simon Daley; **256** AC Cooper; **259** AC Cooper;
260 Gordon Smith/Simon Daley; **267** Darrell Ireland;
269 Bob Wagner/Simon Daley; **272** Shutterstock/
Eduard Kyslynskyy; **280** Public Domain; **283** Ian
Garlick; **286–287** Shutterstock/Porojnicu Stelian;
309 Shutterstock/Daxiao Productions;
314 Shutterstock/Uber Images; **321** Gordon
Smith/Shutterstock/sumire8; **325** Shutterstock/
James Steidl; **332–333** Shutterstock/JDS

Contents

Foreword

When I took up music composition, I used the same textbook as Mozart, *Gradus ad Parnassum*. Mozart referred to it as "simple rules" and, in the hands of the master, they were. The "simple practices and principles" David Gluckman sets out in this book are much the same. They should certainly be used but do not expect similar results.

A successful brand innovator is unlikely to achieve more than one winner in a lifetime. I am not sure how many, of the nine or so noted in this book, Gluckman would rate as outright winners but there are more than enough to make his contribution to the global drinks market truly unique.

Gluckman is too modest to explain what, practices and principles apart, really made the difference: it was consumer understanding and judgment. Not averse to carrying out the odd focus group to enhance his consumer empathy, he also had a healthy instinct for discarding what he thought irrelevant. Similarly, his ability to pick the right package designer and then achieve the elegant design the brand needed is second to none. I know. I've briefed many perfectly good designers and been rewarded with work which was shoddy or indifferent.

Judgment is not something you get from rules, simple or otherwise, nor from experience. Like Mozart, you have it or you don't.

Big corporations, however good at marketing, are widely seen to be poor brand innovators. That is because they do a number of daft things. New brand development builds on experience, yet large companies hand it to their youngest brand managers on the grounds that they are more likely to be original. Most composers create their greatest music later in life. Big companies have complex innovation processes, like 'stage gate', excessive research, analysis paralysis, expensive launches and the committee culture that more or less guarantee failure. Gluckman's client, IDV, had the wit to retain a small company culture within the big corporation.

*"That S*it Will Never Sell!"* is not just a fascinating tale of how these interesting brands came about, but a guide for all those seeking to create new brands. These guidelines will not guarantee success but following them will definitely improve the odds.

Tim Ambler
Senior Fellow, Retired, London Business School

Prologue
Has the Pope ever had a Baileys?

What really scares me is a party where the only people I know are the host and hostess. I'm a bit late and I walk into a room full of people, maybe 20 or 30. Everyone is going at it full tilt and all the separate cliques of friends have formed into tight little groups which appear almost impenetrable. How am I going to join in? How will I look cool and at ease when I am all on my own and don't know a soul? It is a truly daunting experience.

Then rescue: the host appears, he's been pouring drinks, and he forcibly insinuates me into a small group of men and women. "This is my friend David," he says, "He has a really interesting job." "Oh my God", I think to myself, "Not again," and then out it comes. As instructed by our host, one of the group asks me what I do for a living. Someone has to ask. It's been set up by the person giving us his drinks.

"Actually this may surprise you" I respond with a look of enthusiasm bordering on the manic. "I'm an..... undertaker. I run a small family business that has been established in the profession for over 80 years. It was started by my grandfather." My audience looks utterly nonplussed. Remember, we have just met and it's London, one of the centres of the universe.

I begin to warm to the story and the tempo quickens. "It's a really exciting business to be in and I'd like to think that we are a forward-looking company, always experimenting with new ideas. We've recently introduced a 'Burial at Sea' package, out of Newhaven on the Sussex coast, and it's really taking off. We think it's a major growth area in these ecology-conscious times."

The momentum builds and my eyes gleam. My audience becomes morbidly fascinated. Or are they embarrassed? I try to keep within the boundaries of good taste and omit to discuss my disappointment at the failure of bird flu to help us achieve our forecasts. They remain quietly flabbergasted.

But, of course, none of this is true though I did try it once at a drinks party outside London where I was confident that I would never meet any of the other guests again.

This is what really happens.

"And what work do you do, David?" asks a mildly-interested fellow reveller. "Well, it's a rather strange occupation" I reply diffidently, hoping to cut the conversation off at the knees, or that someone will interrupt with a tray of canapés. But no such luck. So with all the enthusiasm of someone on the verge of root canal work, I mutter "I invent drinks."

"You invent drinks?" is the usual puzzled reply. "Do you mean cocktails? Are you some kind of barman who has this lab where you experiment with exotic concoctions? Or do you invent soft drinks like Red Bull? Are there any drinks you've invented that I might have heard of? This is really weird."

By now I am becoming pretty embarrassed by the whole thing – which is why I invented the whole undertaker get-out ploy. But I reluctantly soldier on.

"Well, actually, I invented Baileys. You know, Baileys Irish Cream. I did that back in 1973." If one of the unfortunate listening group is a woman – and this is based on actual past experience – she is likely to respond something like this : "Oh-my-God. Baileys. My mother absolutely adores it. Did you hear that, Jocasta? This man invented Baileys. It's unreal. I don't believe it. He must be terribly rich. Baileys Cream. Wow!"

And it's not as if these rather posh people really adore Baileys. Or even hold it in the same esteem as, say, an obscure Islay single malt or a fine white burgundy from Meursault. Not a bit of it. They might have respected it years ago but most people of legal drinking age regard Baileys as a bit naff. It comes in loads of flavours, at Christmas it sells in Tesco for under a tenner a bottle and a call for a Baileys in a smart West End bar is hardly likely to register you as one of the 'beautiful people'. Chic it ain't. Offering a Baileys after dinner doesn't make it as a fashion statement.

By now the conversation has developed a life of its own and I become surrounded by people who start asking me about other drinks I have created. If they are over a certain age then Aqua Libra will ring a few bells. And Purdey's too, which is still around today. Le Piat D'Or? Well a few of the older ones remember it. Or, if the group is younger, modern and hip, then drinks like Cîroc – a grape vodka known to the cognoscenti in New York as 'Diddy Juice' – and Tanqueray Ten, the world's first fresh botanical gin, will evince nods of recognition.

Some years back I read somewhere that on 3rd December 2007, Diageo announced the sale of the billionth bottle of Baileys since it was first introduced in 1973. That's a thousand million bottles. And they will have sold at least a further 250 million bottles in the eight years since then bringing the total up to something in the area of 1,250,000,000. That's one hell of a lot of bottles. And if we then assume that every bottle of Baileys delivered eight generous servings that suggests that over 12 billion glasses of Baileys have been poured since it all began.

The next thought was about which people might have tried Baileys. Who might they be? Did Gorbachev and Reagan study a bottle up-close and ask each other "who exactly were R&A Bailey?" Is it macho enough for Putin? Is it in Madonna's bar? Has the Dalai Lama tried it? Or the Pope? And have the Clintons ever snuggled down and sipped a cool Baileys on the rocks after a tough day at the hustings? With more than 12 billion glasses, the possibilities are enormous.

It all came about through a chance meeting with a man called Tom Jago in Stresa on Lake Maggiore in Italy in May 1969. Having muddled through both my academic and working life till the age of thirty, I suddenly found myself presented with the opportunity to do something I really enjoyed – to create new products and, especially, new drinks.

It has been the most thrilling working life. This is my story.

Chapter One
The Irish brief

The initial thought behind Baileys Irish Cream took about 30 seconds. In another 45 minutes the idea was formed. But it was a little more complex than that.

I once asked a designer friend to draw me a cartoon for an article I was doing for a magazine. I briefed him over the telephone and he faxed me a superb cartoon 30 minutes later. I called to thank him and remarked about the speed of his response. "It was too quick. 30 minutes. Wow!" He came back at me fast: "It didn't take 30 minutes. It took 30 years".

Baileys was like that for me. A decade of experience kicked in and delivered a great idea. It wasn't as instant as it seemed.

"What are we going to do about this bloody Irish brief?" I asked, testily, challenging my business partner Hugh to feel some pressure. I was annoyed by his ability to take things a great deal more calmly than I ever did. We'd only been in business together for a month and that alone, I thought, warranted a greater sense of urgency. We had families to support.

"What Irish brief?" he replied. We'd discussed it on Friday last, but Hugh was very good at switching off for the weekend.

"IDV," I reminded him, "International Distillers & Vintners. Its Irish company wants us to create a new drinks brand for export." They hadn't said what kind of drink, just that it should be alcoholic.

The technical people at IDV's research and development department in Harlow had concocted some 'heather and honey' traditional-style liqueurs as a starter but no one was much inspired by them. As usual in those days, there was no written instruction and we described the sparse expression of the company's objectives as the 'Wexford Whisper', so vague was the outline of what they wanted. The only proviso was that we should limit the amount of Irish whiskey we used because IDV didn't have any strong relationships with Irish distilleries and wouldn't be able to control supply of the stuff.

Hugh stared at the ceiling. His morning coffee hadn't kicked in yet and he was a self-confessed slow starter. I was still seething from his languid entrance to the office 90 minutes after mine.

We were, I suppose, unlikely business partners. Hugh Reade Seymour-Davies was a 'toff'. He was a 'gentleman copywriter', educated at Eton and Oxford, and an unapologetic classicist. He could quote all the Latin and Greek greats with real facility and would 'get some Latin in' to documents or labels when I felt we needed to impress some of our more intellectual clients. He was steeped in Shakespeare, admired Beethoven and Mozart certainly, but anything written, composed or painted after about 1830 fell into the category of mid-nineteenth century arrivistes.

I, on the other hand, was most definitely an 'arriviste', having fled South Africa in 1961 aboard the Cape Town Castle to occupy a mattress on a floor in a shared room in Earl's Court. Leaving behind me a possessive Jewish family, I'd escaped to London to make my way in advertising. Just before I left South Africa, where I'd been involved with ads for medicines to cure piles and devising promotions for patent fingernail clippers, I'd read Martin Mayer's book *Madison Avenue, U.S.A.* about the explosion of the ad industry in New York and on which the current hit TV series Mad Men has surely drawn.

If the sexy and successful Don Draper had been invented then, he would have been my role model. Well, I smoked as much as he does. Like me he had come from a back-water to the glittering city lights to take his chance in the exciting new world of post-war consumerism in which, after so many years of rationing, even Britain would be open to new and exotic things to eat, drink, drive or wear.

Having spent the sixties as an account executive   also known as a 'suit' – in various advertising agencies, I had managed a transformation to become a product development consultant. That is what brought me to Dean Street.

A leap in the dark
A wacky idea to take to people I'd never met

It was now 1973, twelve years after my arrival in England and Hugh and I had set up on our own in an office that looked out onto the garish sex parlours in the heart of Soho. It was the throbbing neon heart of creative London in those days. *Private Eye*, the satirical magazine, was

Piccadilly Circus, London, circa 1973, 328 paces from our office on Dean Street where Baileys happened.

in full swing, Ronnie Scott's jazz club was the place to go and there were TV production houses and recording studios on every corner.

You could spot local luminaries such as Peter Cook and Richard Ingrams in the modestly appointed pub The Coach and Horses. Barrow boys walked alongside painters like Francis Bacon, lunched on cheap oysters and propped up the same bars, feeding off each other. Jeffrey Bernard was in very good health. Friday afternoons would be celebrated with champagne in Gaston Berlemont's French Pub, aka The York Minster, in Dean Street.

Much of these first weeks had been taken up with furnishing the office, buying materials and writing to a host of people who might become potential clients. It was exciting but also quite daunting.

Hugh looked at me with an almost earnest stare. "What would happen if we mixed Irish whiskey and cream?" he said. "That might be interesting."

Business wasn't exactly streaming in. The early pressure was beginning to tell and I'd been in the office that day since 8am.

We chatted aimlessly for a few minutes about the Irish Brief and then I raised the issue of my previous Irish involvement. "Can we take anything from my Kerrygold butter experience?" I said. (I was in the team that created the Kerrygold brand in the early 1960s.) "Is there something in Ireland's reputation for dairy produce that we can apply to an alcoholic drink – all those lush green rain-sodden pastures and contented cows?"

Hugh looked at me with an almost earnest stare. "What would happen if we mixed Irish whiskey and cream?" he said. "That might be interesting." He sat back and waited for a response.

During my career I visited distilleries in Scotland, Kentucky, Canada and Ireland. Occasionally these trips paid off.

"Let's try it," I replied. Where Hugh was more likely to intellectualise and think through the appalling consequences of dropping cream into Ireland's beloved whiskey, I was all for doing it there and then. I jumped up, almost grabbed him by the lapels and marched him out into the street and into what was then International Stores at the southern end of Berwick Street market in the middle of Soho. It was the nearest supermarket to our office.

We bought a small bottle of Jamesons Irish Whiskey and a tub of single cream and hurried back. It was a lovely May morning. 1973. We mixed the two ingredients in our kitchen, tasted the result and it was certainly intriguing, but in reality bloody awful. Undaunted, we threw in some sugar and it got better, but it still missed something.

We went back to the store, searching the shelves for something else, found our salvation in Cadbury's Powdered Drinking Chocolate and added it to our formula. Hugh and I were taken by surprise. It tasted really good. Not only this, but the cream seemed to have the effect of making the drink taste stronger, like full-strength spirit. It was extraordinary.

THE WHOLE PROCESS had taken about 45 minutes, from the moment Hugh looked at me to the moment we poured our mixture into a cleaned-out screw-top Schweppes' tonic bottle and I called Tom Jago, our client at IDV. I suggested that we meet immediately. I went on my own. Either Hugh had had second thoughts and decided that the gentry at IDV would cast out our muddy concoction with suitable disdain – or he didn't have an available suit hanging up in the office. I suspect it was the latter. Ten minutes later I was in a cab heading for 1 York Gate, an elegant Georgian house in the outer circle of London's beautiful Regent's Park.

In the cab I tried to bring some logic to this wacky idea. Apart from the great taste, which triggered the thought that 'alcoholic drinks don't have to taste punishing', I was interested in our serendipitous discovery that the drink tasted stronger than it really was. I think our original mix was,

Called to the bar
Meeting Major Tom

I was working for an ad agency at the time that counted soap powder
and fish finger manufacturers among its clients. The symposium had
been deadly dull, except for one bright moment when a German delegate
asked why Domestos claimed to kill '99 per cent of all known Germans'.
The actual advertisement said 99 per cent of all known germs.

Tom was the star guest and being one of the few English speakers in
the group, I was given the task of taking him out to dinner. My boss had
issued me with the instructions not to spare on expenses as Tom was 'in
the wine trade' – and these people expected to be entertained lavishly. It
was a challenge to a callow young South African like me. Tom Jago was
tall and handsome, in his late 40s, and he wore his suits well. Born in
Cornwall, the son of a Camelford bank manager, he'd been a protégé of
the Oxford University luminary A.L. Rowse.

On first acquaintance I found him quite formidable. But, as I discovered
over the years I worked with him, he had a good heart, a wonderful sense
of humour and great intelligence and vision. It was more like working with
a friend than a client.

We dined well, as per briefing, and I prudently let him choose the wine.
We sat up at the bar after dinner looking over the complex array of
continental products on offer with their idiosyncratic labels. It was like
being in a kind of art gallery. I loved the heritage and heraldry of it all:
monks beavering away making liqueurs, widows fermenting champagne
and black and white dogs selling whisky; exotic names like Himbeergeist
and Poire Williams and the curious case of the bat on the Bacardi bottle.
Tom was full of wonderful stories about the drinks business that really
captivated me. And we managed to sample a few of the more unusual
offerings along the way.

As the end of the evening approached I remembered that I was helping
to run a new group in the advertising agency where I worked and we were
looking for business. I have never been the world's most comfortable
hustler, but it wasn't too difficult asking Tom if he might consider giving us
some consultancy work. What a change from washing powder, cooking
fat and chicken nuggets it would be.

very roughly, 25% alcohol by volume. Maybe it could be pitched against stronger liqueurs like Tia Maria, where it would appear to be as strong, but would attract much lower duty. It could therefore be more profitable. I was excited. Very excited. Convinced we'd cracked the Irish Brief.

We had just started out as an independent business a few weeks earlier and I don't think we took in that this was an imperative brief that had to be solved in a hurry. It was just something that cropped up in a casual conversation with Tom. We saw nothing in writing. I was to discover some time later, a lot later, that Gilbeys of Ireland management had reached an agreement with the Irish Finance Minister that export earnings on the new brand would be tax exempt for a period of ten years. I seem to recall that at the time of the Baileys' tenth anniversary party – and it was some party – the company had sold about 4 million cases the previous year. Who needed a written brief?

When I got to York Gate I went in to see Tom. I'd first met him in Italy on the shores of Lake Maggiore, which may sound exotic except for the fact that we were both there for a Unilever Research symposium back in 1969.

Now, a few years later, here I was in his office presenting our mucky brown liquid in its recycled bottle with huge enthusiasm. He liked it immediately. Over the years I have come to the conclusion that the real heroes of ideas are not the people who have them – they are the people who buy them. Tom could easily have said, "Sorry old chap, but it's not our sort of thing" – which it really wasn't, given the strong focus on wine, sherry, and 'serious' spirits like gin, whisky and vodka at IDV. But he was as excited as we were about our 'Heath Robinson' product.

Tom and I went for a curry in Drummond Street, near Euston Station. Given the totally revolutionary nature of the product, and the fact that nothing like it had ever been made before, we decided that we would develop it completely before we showed it to the Irish. This was odd coming from both Tom Jago and me, as we were both terribly impatient. (His attention span was not of heroic proportions and I once considered petitioning for the word 'jago' to become adopted as a unit of measurement for attention deficit syndrome). But in this instance we had to take our time about it: there were too many imponderables about our creation. It could turn out to be a very tough sell. Or no sell at all.

We took it to the technical group in Harlow, which is in Essex, about 40 miles north of London, a few days later to present it to Alan Simpson, who ran the division, and his second-in-command, Mac Macpherson. They were 'boffins' or 'techies' and knew about the science of drink production. Mac was in a white coat while Alan looked like the proprietor of a fine wine emporium. "Good suit" I thought. I stood in Alan's office with our precious bottle burning a hole in my raincoat pocket. I was eager for him to taste it there and then. He wasn't quite so keen and when I read his lips the words "later perhaps" seemed to form.

"After lunch" he said and steered us towards a burgundy tasting. Oh dear. He was a wine man at heart. It didn't help that I managed to get quite a bit of wine over my tie and the style of my spitting left much to be desired.

THEY FINALLY TASTED our concoction after lunch – after a bottle of decent red – and there was no doubt, by the expression on their faces, that they thought it was quite disgusting. It wasn't a fine wine after all. It didn't look like wine. It didn't look like any known liqueur and it didn't even taste like whiskey. What was it? We'd gambled on the fact that they might like the taste, but it was evident that they did not. Perhaps it had aged in the five days since we made it.

Yet strangely Mac looked up to us from his awful beige-streaked glass and nodded almost imperceptibly. Whatever we were doing, no matter what he thought of the taste, he knew what we were aiming for. Just a nod, that's all he gave us. Not a 'yes' but better than a 'no'. Mac would be the man who would have to run with this. And he did.

IDV
Gentleman adventurers

Most of this book is about a company called IDV (International Distillers & Vintners). Their offices were at 1 York Gate off London's Regent's Park and their factory was in Harlow, Essex. Their history has been chronicled elsewhere.

Having worked for them since 1969 I was always struck by how gentlemanly they were. Their senior people were totally unlike the more aggressive types I had met in the 'supermarket' product business. They were civilised, urbane, upper class men who created a climate for very adventurous ideas. Aside from Tom Jago, members of their management who spring to mind are Jasper Grinling, Robin Kernick, George Bull, Geoffrey Palau and Tim Ambler. Tim features prominently later in this book.

Much as I would like to take credit for having created the innovative climate within IDV, it wouldn't be true. The company was producing great brands long before I arrived. I'd like to think that I helped perpetuate their spirit over the years that I worked for them.

One of their brands, developed shortly before I started working for them, provided a template for a lot of the work that followed. It was a brilliantly simple piece of 'inside-the-box' innovation called Croft Original – the world's first pale cream sherry.

In the beginning there was Harveys Bristol Cream, a dark, rich, sweet cream sherry. It was hugely popular in the UK after the war, a perfect 'Joan Hunter-Dunn'* pre-prandial tipple. One can imagine gentlefolk in the Home Counties enjoying a glass of deliciously sweet sherry on evenings 'furnish'd and burnish'd by Aldershot sun'. It seemed the quintessentially English drink. And Harveys Bristol Cream represented the apotheosis of that occasion.

Harveys even managed to make inroads into the tough US market and through brilliant advertising it became a drink to be reckoned with. It was the sophisticated cocktail for the emerging New Woman who might have smoked Virginia Slims ('You've come a long way, baby!') or flown with Braniff airlines ('If you've got it, flaunt it!'). These were ad campaigns created by the legendary Mary Wells who aggressively targeted the new upwardly mobile executive woman in the late sixties.

But the gentlemen at IDV had other ideas. They had a sherry company in their bundle called Croft which also owned a companion port lodge in Oporto. They decided to aim Croft at big bad Harveys and shake up the UK sherry market in the process. And they did it with remarkable finesse and simplicity. Someone in the pharmaceutical industry once said "if you want to make money out of a new cure, create a new disease". And that is what IDV, with the help of their advertising agency, Young & Rubicam, managed to do.

The 'disease' IDV created was 'lack of sophistication'. They argued that dark sherry overtly signalled sweet sherry. And sweet sherry wasn't sophisticated. They offered the perfect panacea. It was called pale cream sherry and its name was Croft Original. It was not significantly drier than Harveys and both were complex well-crafted products. These companies had been making sherry for hundreds of years.

But Croft Original looked dry. It looked more sophisticated. And to clinch their argument they enlisted the help of two of England's most beloved literary figures, Bertie Wooster and his butler, the omniscient Jeeves. Jeeves was an arbiter of good taste and a staunch advocate for Croft Original. He was responsible for keeping the occasionally wayward Wooster on the straight and narrow and up to standard.

What an unbelievably simple idea: a cream (sweet) sherry that looked like a dry sherry. It managed to cut Harveys' business in half and turn Croft into an important contributor to IDV's profit.

The brand's the thing
Baileys comes to life

Although IDV didn't have the technology to mix alcohol and cream together, Tom insisted that the team apply resources to studying it. The technical challenge was under way and Tom was now in a hurry to do the branding: the bottle, the label and the name.

I remembered once, during the Kerrygold days, being told by a well-known Irishman that so many Irish names sound quaint when applied to brands. His name was Tony O'Reilly and O'Reilly's Irish Cream might indeed have sounded a bit whimsical. I could see what he meant and it had stuck in my mind. We needed what they called an 'Anglo-Irish' name. We were sure that a family name might be better than a 'thing' or a place name. That was the popular convention of the business in those days. After all, many drinks were named after the people who made them.

As the office that Hugh and I shared in Dean Street was only temporary accommodation, we were planning a move within Soho. Hugh insisted that we had an office close to a game butcher's – in this case Parrish & Fenn. He liked his new season grouse. We visited some premises in nearby Greek Street, alongside a pub called The Pillars of Hercules and above a restaurant of no fixed ethnicity that was called Baileys Bistro.

We were still struggling to find a name for our revolutionary new drink and there it was; above the door. Baileys. Was it really right in front of my face? It was certainly Anglo-Irish and in a flurry of post-rationalisation I managed to dredge up from my memory a dairy of that name in the Port Elizabeth of my youth in South Africa. This gave it a kind of relevance in my head. I called Tom: "How about Baileys Irish Cream?" I proffered hopefully, "It sounds right, perfect I think".

Without any hesitation he bought the name. He was like that. If he saw an idea and it worked for him he could be very quick on the draw. We designated it an 'Irish Cream Chocolate Liqueur'. Names can be tough and often really easy to reject with a comment like "I just don't like it". Being words, not graphic designs, they are within everyone's purview so anyone can reject them. Getting to Baileys as quickly as we did was unusual. Indeed, as I discovered in later years, it was incredible.

A few weeks later I telephoned my mother. "Was there a dairy in Port Elizabeth called Baileys back in the early days? I'm sure I can remember it." "No" she said "Definitely not". There went our brand's 'certificate of provenance'. I would have to settle for Messrs. Chesterman and Cymberg, owners of Baileys Bistro and our future landlords. Not an especially Irish pair.

The next step was packaging, and we needed a bottle. Not being confident enough in the overall idea to suggest spending money on a new mould which could have run to several thousand pounds, we looked around for an existing bottle and Tom found one for an Irish whiskey brand that the company distributed called Redbreast. We decided we'd use that.

It was brown glass, squat and round like a typical liqueur bottle and seemed very appropriate for Baileys. But there was a problem: it had a prominent 'R' embossed on the shoulder of the bottle. I guess we could have changed Baileys to a name beginning with 'R', but Baileys was now fixed in our minds and it would have been hard to change. We had started to use it in conversation.

We also had to give it an address, so the very first label carried the legend 'The Dairy Distillery, County Monaghan'. It was a complete fabrication of mine – but it sounded good. And very Kerrygold.

Hugh and I had a secretary called Amy Wagner. Her husband Bob was a graphic designer and they lived on a small boat on the Thames at Kingston. Rather than drag Bob all the way in to London when he could be working, I wrote out a design brief and asked Amy to show it to him and get him to submit some designs as soon as he could. The brief asked for Kerrygold butter styling – but for an alcoholic drink: contented grazing cows and lush green pastures– we wanted an Irish rustic idyll on a label.

A couple of days later Bob delivered. I think in those early times he was paid five guineas a design and he had sent about twenty for us to choose from. Amy laid them out on our table and Tom, Hugh and I looked them over and immediately lit on one. That was it. We even liked the streaky magic marker khaki that was the dominant colour.

It was pretty close to the Baileys label that you see today, give or take several tweaks and many millions of pounds over the last forty years. These were still early days in our product development lives and there was a huge buzz seeing an idea begin to assume a physical form. I was no designer so depended on other people to perform this magic.

We had another cunning plan. Let's not rush to Dublin with their new drink yet. Let's show the Baileys bottle with a printed label. In those days we usually dealt in rough designs rendered with crayons and magic marker pens. There were no computers to produce perfect facsimiles of the real thing. We felt that showing Baileys as a rough design would make it look like a tentative idea: one which people would want to change and modify. We wanted Baileys to look irresistibly authentic.

Market research
Use it or (as we did) lose it

The liquid product itself started to take shape in the June and July of 1973 but there were two other things we wanted to do before making the journey to Dublin. We would set up some focus groups, in which we would present Baileys in a proper bottle – as if it already existed – and ask real potential customers what they thought about it. That would be the theoretical world.

Secondly, we would put a couple of bottles into a bar and see if anyone actually asked for it and paid for a glass. That would be the real world. It was small stuff really. In those days market research was not the all-powerful force it is today, and it certainly wasn't in the drinks

Bob Wagner's first design. Note the 'magic marker effect' in the khaki colouring.

trade. But we thought it would make us look professional when we went to Dublin for the Big Sell. Cream and chocolate with Irish whiskey needed all the help it could get.

When the night of the focus group came, I looked nervously around the room. This was the male group. But then these were men who were prepared to turn up for a free drink and get paid for it. We showed them the bottle that we were so proud of and began pouring out the glasses. Among most groups of drinking men there's always one who seems to dominate proceedings – you know who he is, he's the one who sits right in front of the interviewer and talks the loudest. It was vital for us to have him on our side and I kept my eye on him for his reaction. He drank it down, and then the researcher asked him what he thought.

"I'm a pint drinker," he said, looking down at his schooner. "And when I've had enough beer I move to shorts, like Scotch or vodka."

Oh dear. To make matters worse, being a talker, he went on: "It's a girl's drink," he said. There was an outbreak of nods and echoes of agreement among the other men. After this what man was going to openly lay claim to liking 'a girl's drink'? It was an absolute no-no. But when we looked at their glasses every one of them had been drained. It might not have been their kind of drink, but there was nothing wrong with the taste.

The Allsop Arms today.

The women's group, on which we were now relying, wasn't really any more encouraging. One of them said "It looks and tastes like Kaolin & Morphine", which was a popular medicine for diarrhoea (it's still around).

So the research didn't deliver a hugely successful result and I didn't feel totally confident about making the trip to Dublin on the back of it. Mind you, it was unlikely that IDV's Irish team would have been considered as research-obsessives back then. Concurrent with this

---

I'd call in bright with hope, smile at the landlord and say, "Any sales yet?" He would shake his head slowly and carry on cleaning his pint pots."

'exhaustive' market research (three focus groups) we also had our real world test: two bottles behind the bar at the Allsop Arms just north of the Marylebone Road. I'd chosen this pub particularly because it was on my way home from Tom's office at York Gate.

I'd call in bright with hope, smile at the landlord and say, "Any sales yet?" He would shake his head slowly and carry on cleaning his pint pots as the two un-opened bottles glowered down at me from their place on the shelf. I wondered if that was where our Baileys would forever stay, getting dustier and duller, having travelled only a few streets up from the offices of IDV. Then I called in one evening and one of the bottles had gone. It looked like the landlord would no longer give our Baileys shelf space but "Oh no," he said. "Two policemen came in this afternoon and demolished the whole bottle between them."

"Right!" I said to myself. That was the incontrovertible evidence we were seeking. "Dublin, here we come…"

Chapter Two
Baileys was it – there was no Plan B

One of the abiding beliefs in my life as a
product developer was that you should
always go for a single idea. In this case,
Baileys, an outrageously different kind of drink,
was it. There was no Plan B. That became the
template for everything I did in the future.
   When you think about it, it's pretty easy to
come up with a number of plausible solutions
to a brief. But you are not committing yourself.
You are leaving the decision to someone else.
As a consultant and a specialist in the field,
a purely speculative approach to ideas is
an abdication of one's responsibility.

It was mid-November, dark, wet and cold. 1973. We collected the Baileys report from the market researcher alongside the Chiswick roundabout en route to Heathrow. We were cutting it fine for our big Dublin meeting. Tom drove and I leafed through the document in the car. It wasn't a comfortable read.

"This isn't going to help our case" I said. "It's not all bad, but it isn't all good either." The bit about being a 'girly drink' was in there and so was the comment likening it to Kaolin & Morphine. It was perfect ammunition for someone who wanted to kill the idea. The report contained nothing to reflect the earth-shattering idea we thought Baileys was now that we observed it in its full packaged glory.

"Why don't we just put it away and not mention it?" I said. Tom immediately agreed and I stuck it in my briefcase and left it there. It stayed in my briefcase until 1984 when I unveiled it at the 10th anniversary party. It got a huge laugh. The 'Kaolin & Morphine-flavoured girly drink' had sold about four million cases (48 million bottles) that year.

The weather in Dublin was as miserable as in London. We were met at the airport and driven to the Gilbeys' offices in the Naas Road, a dreary industrial district outside Dublin. I was excited rather than concerned. We had our kit: a couple of bottles of product that had been through the Research & Development mill at Harlow - so it was vaguely shelf stable - and three fully-dressed bottles complete with beautifully printed labels and gold wax seals on the shoulders of the bottles which Tom had fashioned in his shed at home. They looked terrific and they looked real. We were relying on these bottles to clinch the sale.

Showtime - at last.

Making it 'real' worked
They loved it – and better still, they bought it!

Gilbeys of Ireland was a smallish outpost of the IDV empire. Most of the companies abroad at that stage were called Gilbeys after the founding fathers, the Gilbey family, who originally ran a coaching business in Essex in the 19th century. They were great Victorian traders and set up outposts across the British Empire. Gilbeys had a production plant where it bottled brands such as Smirnoff vodka and Gilbey's gin. It also distributed Croft Original sherry and J&B whisky along with a large portfolio of wines. It was pretty successful for a small offshoot of a large international company.

Its main reason for commissioning a new product for export was that the Irish government had started giving generous subsidies for brands that were shipped to new markets across the world and Gilbeys wanted to capitalise on that. Because Ireland was then almost exclusively an agricultural economy, products with locally grown ingredients were even better.

The Irish team, headed by their chief executive, David Dand, weren't hard-core, button-down 1970s marketing types with smart suits, matching shirts and ties and cylindrical slide rules. They were a friendly-looking bunch; guys that you might meet at a golf club or in the snug bar at the Shelbourne. In fact, David Dand wasn't very Irish at all; he had an accent that was light Dublin with a sprinkling of Manchester or Leeds. He was a bit 'tweedy'. Keith McCarthy-Morrogh, the marketing director, was Irish upper class and could have been a character from *The Irish RM* by Somerville and Ross. With rakish curly hair greying at the temples, he and his Prince of Wales check suit were made for each other.

Doing a joint presentation with Tom was always challenging since he rarely stuck to the script and invariably stole most of my lines. Despite our somewhat unorthodox double-act Tom and I managed a persuasive pitch for the Baileys idea. To help things along I cited my Kerrygold experience. Kerrygold was important to me and one of the keys to the development of Baileys. By that time the famed gold-wrapped butter had been celebrated as one of the European business successes of the 1960s and my association with it, I hoped, would add a bit of weight to our argument. I think it did.

Kerrygold Butter
Where Baileys (sort of) began

Back in the early 'sixties when I was working for the London advertising agency Benton & Bowles, we had been approached by An Bord Bainne (The Irish Dairy Board) to help it brand Irish butter. This had been no mean task. Up until that time Irish butter had no profile; it was used as an unnamed component in blended butters to emerge on supermarket shelves in dull wrappers as an anonymous own label product. Its lack of identity meant it could never command a decent market price.

Benton & Bowles created the hugely successful Kerrygold brand and I had been a junior member of the team. This experience gave me a sense of Ireland and Irishness and that knowledge provided the template from which Baileys was drawn. The operation was headed at the Irish end by A J F 'Tony' O'Reilly, one of the most charismatic people I have ever met. A British Lions rugby star, he was later to become president of Heinz in the US, owner of the *Irish Independent* and other newspapers and one of the richest men in Ireland

Our foreplay over, the Irish team responded enthusiastically. They handled our bottle respectfully and even savoured the Baileys product to which Mac had applied considerable finesse since our initial 'International Stores' effort. Much to my relief they didn't even ask if we had done any market research. It wasn't an issue in those days.

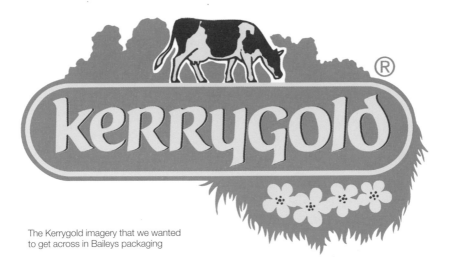

The Kerrygold imagery that we wanted to get across in Baileys packaging

Lunch was pretty lavish, with several bottles of wine going down – and very good wine at that. Perrier hadn't become fashionable then, so people were still content to do real drinking at lunch time. We were in the wine trade after all. I suspect that the word went out to upgrade the vintages when they realised that we had delivered something that they really liked. A couple of bottles of Ducru Beaucaillou of a reputable year appeared and disappeared swiftly.

I'm sure we had sworn everyone to secrecy on our side of the Irish Sea so that Baileys was a 'cold pitch' to David and his colleagues. No one in Dublin knew what to expect from us. But the 'Wexford Whispers' were out and when I retired to the men's room I came across Tom Keaveney, the Gilbeys sales director.

He had not been at our pitch nor was he invited to the lunch but, via some magical Irish leprechaun osmosis hotline, he knew about Baileys and the details of our presentation. We occupied adjacent troughs in the management washroom. He looked across at me – we'd never met before – and muttered "I've heard about your idea."

"Oh yes?" I replied. "It's not for the Irish market. Definitely not," he said. "It'll never sell here." Somewhat chastened, I returned to the port and Stilton.

On reflection, it was quite an event, especially since we'd gone to Dublin with a single idea: there was no Plan B and we didn't have any other ideas to offer. David Dand and his merry men could have squashed Baileys in an instant had they not liked it or felt it wasn't their kind of thing but these friendly, clubby Irishmen in their backwater offices in an industrial suburb of Dublin had the balls to say 'yes'.

And it was not without risk: they knew full-well that they would have to build a plant to make it, they would have to invest in bottling lines and they would have to spend some real money on marketing. They were not a huge company, and it would strain their resources.

Taking ownership of the idea
Baileys becomes both royal and ancient

No matter how well an idea is received, it is a complex entity and changes are inevitably made. The Baileys team now had to make its own imprint. The first thing they did was to remove the word 'chocolate' from the description Irish Cream Chocolate Liqueur. In those days, in the early 1970s, the word 'chocolate' did not sit comfortably on the label of a premium liqueur brand. It also made the idea easier to copy. We were pretty happy with that decision. Nowadays things are different. The notion of 'Kandy Coloured Tangerine Flake Triple-Distilled' vodka from Vietnam would pass without anyone turning a hair.

As soon as they started making an imprint on this strange new idea they began to assume ownership. And once they owned it they would commit to it. But they were respectful enough to keep us informed of changes. And ask for our help when they needed it.

I got a call from David Dand in early July of 1974. It was about 9am and I was reading the sports page of *The Guardian* in the office. "I'm worried about the name," he said. "Oh my God" I thought. "We can't

The 'Kaolin & Morphine-flavoured girly drink' had sold about four million cases (48 million bottles) that year."

Brand Baileys Original Irish Cream

USP World's first cream liqueur

Client David Dand, Gilbeys of Ireland

Taste Chocolate cream

Ideal drinker Everyone - we hadn't a clue

Launched November 1974

Designer Bob Wagner

do another name now. It will take forever to get it through." My heart sank. David went on, "No, I don't mean Baileys. It's just that we can't just call it Baileys. It needs a first name or at least an initial."

I looked down at the paper and there was an article about a golf tournament. The Open was being played at Royal Lytham. The headline mentioned R&A, golf's governing body, and I instantly blurted "How about two initials? How do you like the sound of R&A Bailey? Think golf and the R&A." "Great" he said, "I love it." And that was that and I went back to reading the paper.

Yet as I thought about it after our conversation, a fantasy began to form in my mind. I could see them: R & A Bailey were two brothers, one a distiller and the other a dairy farmer. They had disliked each other for decades. Their father looked to bring them together as he reached his dotage. He had a huge estate and wanted to keep it in the family. So he said to his sons "If you can find a way of working together, I'll leave you all my land".

They sat down one night to try to work things out. A lot of whiskey went down when Robert, somewhat the worse for wear, mistakenly added some of his brother Aidan's cream to his tipple. He tried it and loved it. They made up and the rest is history.

Well that was my personal story. It helped to bring the idea to life for me. I had never intended for it to be used in public as it was a pure fiction. Interestingly, the 'Mr R and Mr A' idea was the theme for one of the early TV commercials for Baileys in the UK. It was pretty tame and utterly unbelievable, which goes to show that not all fantasies work in the real world.

Another 'Baileys moment' was the discovery of an attractive, traditional restaurant in Dublin called The Bailey. I could imagine our drink being enjoyed there a long time ago. It gave a gentle nudge of support to our off-the-wall idea.

One of the serendipitous aspects of the Baileys development came from the fact that IDV had very recently been taken over by Maxwell Joseph's Grand Metropolitan Hotels group and it in turn also owned Express Dairies – and Express was a significant player in the Irish market. That meant that the cream that would go into Baileys could be bought not on the open market but from our own company.

We had inadvertently stumbled on the idea of the management theory called 'Vertical Integration' and, while it wasn't a completely new phenomenon in commercial circles, it was new to us. Even the original Baileys plant was based on a second-hand homogeniser bought from Express.

Countdown to launch
Ask the expert

We were building up to the Baileys launch which would be held at Tailor's Hall in Dublin in November 1974. During the early part of that month I had occasion to visit New York on a job and Tom asked me to take a trip to Chicago to show Baileys to a colourful friend of his called Max 'the Hat' Zimmerman. Max owned the largest liquor store in Chicago, or in his words, the 'largest liquor store on the planet'.

Tom felt that America would be important for Baileys and since we'd both met Zimmerman earlier that year (see page 49), it would make sense to canvass his opinion. Mind you, that kind of thing could come back to bite you. What if Max didn't like it? Bad news could spread. But we were confident that we had a big idea so the decision was "Go for it".

New York 1974. Where
Baileys started life as
'The Impossible Cream'

Storming the Zimmerman citadel
Fat chance

I flew from La Guardia to Chicago at 7 am. It was cold in New York and the windy city was colder still. I took a cab to Zimmerman's Liquor Store in the Loop and got there by mid-morning. But when I entered the store Max greeted me brusquely, as if we'd never clapped eyes on each other. I was just another salesman storming the Zimmerman citadel. Max was shrouded in a cloak of impatience. "What have you got?" he said.

I said it was cold and Baileys was by no means perfected even this close to its launch. I showed Max the bottle. He looked at it, stony-faced. I opened the cap and started to pour it into a glass I had brought for the occasion. Max showed nary a flicker. He looked at the bottle, gimlet-eyed. The liquid wouldn't pour. It refused to leave the bottle. The cold had got to it.

I could now almost smell Max's impatience. I grabbed a pencil from his desk and unceremoniously penetrated the opening in the bottle. Out came Baileys in random globs, some into the glass and some over Max's desk. I had a heavy cold so was well-armed with tissues. I cleaned the glass, mopped up the mess on the desk and offered Max a taste.

Given the texture, he sucked at it rather than sipped it, and before I could say 'Heath Rubinstein', I was scuttling out of the door. In my recently-acquired fey wine trade manner, I half expected Max to invite me to lunch to schmooze the old days at Loudenne. Absolutely no chance. Max didn't do lunch on his ticket and definitely not with a third-rate salesman like me on that day.

Back in Dublin, the launch party duly took place, as planned, at Tailor's Hall and those of us from across the water who were present, Tom, Mac, Alan Simpson and me, were told to sit at the back of the hall and keep quiet. Baileys was suddenly no longer our creation – it was theirs – and piqued as we might have been at the time, in hindsight they were right. If Baileys was to succeed, they had to feel that they owned it. I can remember being introduced to someone at the party as "A man who helped out with the label design" and while it rankled, I let it go.

Mixed fortunes
Baileys and lemonade (or 'Gorilla Snot')

One of the strange things about the success of the Baileys venture at that time was that nothing really sank in. We had made a presentation, people liked the idea and then it 'left the building'. We didn't really see it for a year. We got back to the question of solving new problems and looking for other business.

And it was to be about seven years before Baileys really appeared on the radar and looked like a success. I would show it to my sophisticated advertising friends and they thought it was a bit 'Mickey Mouse' and when I offered it up after dinner people usually looked at it sneeringly and said "later perhaps". It lacked the savoir-faire of brands such as Cointreau with its sexy sophisticated ad campaign.

We presented the Baileys idea in 1973, it was launched in 1974 but it was another three years before it began to look like a winner. It was almost long enough for people to forget whose idea it was. I remember attending a few consultants' presentations where the protagonists claimed to have invented Baileys. I managed to keep my cool.

Nor was Baileys universally applauded in the elegant surrounds of 1 York Gate, IDV's head office. I can remember Tom telling me after the launch that someone had described me as having 'the palate of a plumber'. Given that plumbers earned a lot more than I did in those days, I took that as a compliment. People nowadays often ask me how much money we get per bottle sold. My answer is that we were paid about £3,000 all-in for the development – though the company did keep employing me for another 30 years.

In fact, IDV's UK company had a different view of Baileys from that of other companies in the network. Its management saw it as a replacement for the Dutch egg liqueur, Advocaat, which it had distributed in the UK. In its campaign to compete with Advocaat, the first Baileys formulation was mixable with lemonade like an Advocaat 'Snowball'. These were very early days for the formula and Mac and his colleagues were feeling their way.

The mixable Baileys product was a disaster. Cream and fizzy lemonade were uncomfortable bedfellows and the result of the mixture was an almost chewable dirty substance which some malicious barman dubbed 'Gorilla Snot'. Given my limited experience of simian effluents, I was not in a position to judge but the cocktail still exists — though the gorilla act seems to have been cleaned up.

Moment of truth
"That shit will never sell!"

Baileys kicked off in the UK and, perhaps less enthusiastically, in Ireland during 1975. The rest of the world was keeping its powder dry waiting to see what would happen. One encouraging fact was that Baileys was finding its way into executive briefcases as IDV's heavy mob toured the world.

A legendary anecdote in the brand's history is said to have occurred when Anthony Tennant (later knighted) took a bottle of Baileys to Abe Rosenberg, head of the Paddington Corporation in New York. Abe was a titan of the drinks industry and the man who had turned J&B Rare into the biggest selling Scotch in America in the 1960s.

The story goes that he held up the Baileys bottle and looked at it with some disdain. "The green background colour on the label reminds me of US uniforms in Vietnam" he said. He sipped at the muddy brown liquid with absolutely no enthusiasm. And then, it is said, he pronounced the immortal words "That shit will never sell!"

Nevertheless, he launched it into the US later that year with the extraordinary advertising line 'The Impossible Cream'. In the words of S J Perelman in one of his advertising sketches 'the idea had thematic milk'. Despite its esoteric advertising, Baileys rose to become the biggest selling liqueur in the US – and indeed the rest of the world.

That's some good shit.

Australians to the rescue
Baileys all the rage down under

Meanwhile, Baileys had attracted attention in many places, being new and different, but it received its real impetus from an unlikely source – Australia. Whereas the wine and single malt buffs in the UK and Europe still held it at arm's length, the Aussies had few pretensions and the local managing director, after a visit to the Baileys' plant in Dublin, pronounced it in classic Australian fashion "a bloody good drop". He promptly ordered a full container, the contents of which flew off the shelves as soon as it landed. He ordered two more. Baileys became so popular that liquor stores carried signs which said things like 'It'll be here in a week. Place your orders now.' People knew exactly what they meant.

After only five years in the market, Baileys attracted as many as seventy-five competitors round the world. All of them were look-alikes at lower prices and some were even made with wine bases rather than spirit. There was Bayla's in Spain and Baitz' Island Cream in Australia and Irish competitors produced Carolans, O'Darby's and Emmets. Everyone ripped off Bob Wagner's Irish pastoral idyll label design which became the Irish cream graphic generic.

There was also a lot of vigorous activity within IDV to capitalise on the new technology and develop more products. How about a cream from England someone suggested? Together with a US company, Glenmore Distillers from Louisville, Kentucky, we developed Greensleeves, a mint cream liqueur fashioned after the famous confectionery brand After Eight. It was an unmitigated disaster.

"

Test marketed in Chicago, the liquid was hastily put together and emerged looking more like Greysleeves, a decidedly unappetising prospect."

Brand John Dowland's Greensleeves

Name After the song

USP After Eight cream liqueur

Client Bob Farrell, Glenmore Distillers USA

Taste Mint chocolate & cream

Ideal drinker Clearly not Jeeves or Wooster

Test Chicago, 1978

Designer Gerry Barney, Sedley Place

Test marketed in Chicago, the liquid was hastily put together and emerged looking more like Greysleeves, a decidedly unappetising prospect. It was pilloried, sneeringly, in a Bertie Wooster Croft Original commercial where a green cocktail was referred to by Jeeves as 'The Chicago Shock'. That was someone at IDV perhaps envious of Baileys' success. George (later Sir George) Bull, chairman of IDV at the time, vowed never to allow the company to even vaguely consider a green product or label ever again.

After a couple of years the Irish did really believe that they were the only begetters of Baileys, so they decided to develop a cream of their own called Penny Royal. It was test marketed in the North of England. What they had failed to realise was that people in that part of the world regarded the herb Penny Royal as an abortifacient which didn't do much for the idea. Talk about throwing the baby out with the bath water...

Getting famous
Not such a good idea

It was 1982, eight years after launch. Baileys was doing well, selling something like 40 million bottles a year worldwide. We had a call from the BBC. They wanted to interview us for the programme Food & Drink. The interviewer turned out to be none other than Henry Kelly, England's favourite Irishman at the time. It wasn't an easy ride. My experience with the Irish in the past was that it was always a case of 'my country right or wrong'. But Mr Kelly didn't seem to share that view.

On the surface it seemed like a great opportunity for Hugh and me to get some credit for the idea. But in reality it was pretty terrifying. We were railroaded into expressing opinions and there was no opportunity for us to stop and think. Hugh did rather better than I did, but I don't think either of us covered ourselves with glory. It all happened so quickly. I imagined they would say "Are you OK with that?" and then do a retake. Not a chance.

The real meanness happened in the editing suite and when we saw the programme we were gobsmacked. The camera opened on lush Irish pastureland. There was soft accompanying music. The voice-over said "You thought it came from here..." Then cut to a Soho street and

On the surface it seemed like a great opportunity for Hugh and me to get some credit for the idea. But in reality it was pretty terrifying. We were railroaded into expressing opinions and there was no opportunity for us to stop and think."

pan across to show a strip club, a massage parlour and a porno book shop. End on the front door of our office at 6 Greek Street. The voice-over continued "....but it really came from here." It was all intended to discredit Baileys and to call its authentic Irishness into question.

We fought our corner as bravely as we could. Baileys was made in Ireland with Irish ingredients and the people responsible for producing and marketing it were all Irish. Why the attempt to assassinate it, I wondered? In most countries journalists might have praised the Baileys achievement: two guys in a shabby office above a restaurant in Greek Street managing to create a multi-million dollar brand so quickly and for very little money. But no. The tabloid attitude of the BBC really surprised me.

My next brush with the media was rather less contentious. A friend's wife was working for our local paper in North London, the *Ham & High*. She asked if she could do an article on me for her paper and I gladly agreed. It appeared when I was away on vacation.

On my return, I got a call from a friend saying that she had kept a copy of the article and asked if I'd like to collect it at our local pub. When she handed it over she mentioned in revered tones that the radio and TV star Chris Evans was in the pub and asked if I'd like to meet him. I could not think of anything we might have in common so I politely declined. But she was insistent and I was shunted across to meet Chris. The conversation lasted a matter of seconds. We were polite but no intelligible information was exchanged. What could an elderly fellow like me have to interest one of UK talk radio's glitterati? I quietly went home.

Next day at about 3pm I had a call from the daughter of an old friend. "Guess what" she said, "I've been listening to Chris Evans on Radio 2 all morning and most of it was about you. He said that he met this guy in a pub last night who had invented something. He asked people to call in and guess what it was. I realised it was you so I called in, said it was Baileys and won a prize."

It is now 42 years on. Baileys has become the biggest-selling liqueur in the world. It sells about 120 million bottles a year and can be found in bars and liquor stores from Tallahassee to Tbilisi. It's come a long way from International Stores at the bottom end of Berwick Street in Soho. It was a great adventure and there were many, many more adventures to come...

Coming full circle
Kerrygold gets in on the act... 40 years on

As I have said more than once, Baileys, and indeed all the other cream liqueurs in the world owe their existence to Kerrygold Irish butter. It triggered the thought that created a multi-billion dollar market. I was amazed to see the launch in October 2014 of a new liqueur – Kerrygold Irish Cream, done through a partnership between the Irish Dairy Board and US importer Imperial Brands.

The product is described thus: "As the new gold standard of Irish creams, Kerrygold Irish Cream Liqueur expertly blends the finest, freshest Irish cream, aged Irish whiskey and luxurious chocolate. The result is a truly smooth, indulgent sip that will convince any consumer of its superior quality. Crafted with cream from Kerrygold's Irish dairy farms, Kerrygold Irish Cream Liqueur seeks to set a new standard in the category, standing apart from competitors, by delivering more fresh Irish cream and chocolate in every bottle".

The wheel has indeed turned full circle. Even Bob Wagner's classic graphic generic has been played back, cows and all. I am not sure of the logic of this leap from a mid-range everyday product from the chill cabinet to the heady heights of the liqueur shelf. Perhaps research pronounced that it was a smart move. Who knows?

The perfect end to the Baileys story: from butter to booze and back again.

Chapter Three
Winding up
the oenophiles

Wine, especially in the UK, was a tough market to penetrate. In the sixties it was upper class, conservative and well-satisfied. We managed to break in big time with Le Piat d'Or but other ideas were much harder to sell.

When we started, the wines that worked were the ones people could remember next time they were in a store: Blue Nun, Black Tower, Lancers or Mateus. Obscure French names in nondescript bottles were not that easy for the average wine drinker to recall second time round.

The growth of wine has had a kind of Japanese knotweed impact on the alcoholic drinks business since it started to explode at the end of the sixties. Where has all the sherry gone? What happened to Martini – 'The Right One' – and drinks like Dubonnet and Cinzano? Or Babycham, the 'champagne perry' that gave advertising boss Jack Wynne Williams a white Rolls Royce in the 1950s? It was his reward from the company, Showerings, for delivering such a successful idea. Wine seems to have taken up most of the space occupied by all of those drinks. In the UK, a glass of dry white is the new default for many people looking for a casual evening tipple these days.

But it wasn't always like that. In the 1960s wine was a very different and very difficult proposition for most people in places like the UK and even the US.

Aside from the precious posh few who had enjoyed wine at dinner at home, the majority of us were utterly befuddled by the stuff. You'd go into a liquor store to be confronted by an array of similar-looking bottles with similar-looking labels: white backgrounds with black lettering – and all in French. There was nothing to tell you anything about the wines, colour apart, and if you did happen to find a wine that you particularly liked, the chances were that you would forget what you bought the next time you visited a shop.

I looked at a present-day wine list from a well-known supermarket chain and it contained these names: Charte d'Assemblage Pays D'Oc, Terre de Brune Sancerre, Arc du Rhone Chateauneuf du Pape and Chateau Roquefort Roquefortissime and tried to imagine someone in the early seventies trying to make head or tail of what the names and labels meant. Come to think of it, they are pretty complicated now.

Roquefortissime? The nearest I might have come it to it was 'exceedingly cheesy' – but then French is not one of my strong suits.

This overbearing respect for wine, and especially French wine, was summed up by the behaviour of people who came to visit you bringing a bottle to drink at dinner. "We bought this which was recommended by a friend. I hope it's all right." And as I started to become associated with the drinks business, people became even more self-conscious when bringing wine. The offerings became a little more expensive as well. Not that I ever became a wine sophisticate.

The other problem back then was the taste of wine. If you hadn't been taught about wine on your mother's knee you probably hadn't developed a taste for the harsh tannic flavours that characterised most French stuff. Also, they seemed to vary, from year to year and bottle to bottle. "Zis is ze product of our terroire. It is what it is, n'est-ce pas?"

Grappling with the grape
Chateau d'Yquem for lunch, on a Tuesday

I did learn a bit about wine during my advertising days, as we drank quite a lot of it at lunch. One thing someone told me that stuck in my head was that the best place for a wine to be on a list was in the 'third cheapest' slot. If you were entertaining, your guests would know if you ordered the bottom two, but the third one began to vanish into the crowd and could not so easily be recognised. That way you could avoid being seen as a cheapskate.

Back in the ad agency days we had a few clients who really knew their stuff and there were a number of occasions when we would order newly-discovered (by us) Chateau d'Yquem after lunch. (To those who may not be familiar with this wine, it is a Premier Cru Supérieur Sauternes.) I read somewhere that Czar Nicholas II once appropriated the entire vintage of Yquem for one year. In 1964 you could buy it from

Peter Dominic's or Victoria Wines, local London liquor stores, for £2.50 a bottle but it didn't taste quite so good at home. If you want to buy a bottle of 2001 today, you can 'add one to your trolley' for a mere £426.

I wasn't the only person to treat first growth clarets with a measure of disrespect. Chris Patten, writing about his spell as governor of Hong Kong in the period leading up to handover in 1997, said that he had never seen so much fine wine on show as in Hong Kong and Taiwan but that much of it was taken mixed with 7Up.

There were definitely 'wine trade types' at IDV when I started out. They were invariably 'Hooray Henrys' who had been to public school and suckled on Chateauneuf du Pape and Beaume de Venise.

Although an old Etonian and a gent, new managing director Anthony Tennant was less than enamoured with the fine wine ethos that

Stock reduction

One of Tom Jago's more imaginative ploys involved an attempt to auction off a lot of IDV's stock of fine wines to generate some cash during the difficult 1970s. We ran full page ads in *The Times* and the *Financial Times* inviting people to buy ten cases of fine wines for £240 – or £2 per bottle. There was a selection of wines and you could upgrade the quality of your purchase by participating in a fairly simple quiz. I think it was reasonably successful but didn't set the world on fire. But perhaps it was the forerunner of present day Sunday newspaper offers for wine.

In payment for writing the ads – my partner Hugh was the wordsmith here – Tom gave us one tranche of five cases each. I can remember three of the wines: a Sauterne called Chateau Liot, Chateau Ducru Beaucaillou and, the jewel in the crown, Chateau Mouton Rothschild 1972. The last mentioned can be bought these days for over £500 for a single bottle, so I can reflect fondly on taking one of mine to our local 'bring-your-own' Indian restaurant, The Bombay, to impress a girl friend. It created quite a stir with the other diners, especially since it was regaled with the pink paper napkin they used round the neck of the bottle to prevent wine spilling on the tablecloth.

pervaded the corridors of 1 York Gate. Even though he had cut his teeth in the advertising business, he did not really approve of those long, lazy lunches with G&Ts, Meursault and Macon and topped off with a crusty vintage Taylor's or a cool Sauternes.

One of his more memorable utterances was said to be that "Jesus Christ was able to achieve one great miracle, turning water into wine. But the other was beyond him: turning wine into profit". Wine was an agricultural product, subject to the vicissitudes of climate, and aside from the fine stuff, it was hard to make a profit from it. (At £2 a bottle in our newspaper competition Mouton Rothschild 1972 couldn't have been delivering too much profit.)

How can you *invent* a wine?
Make it memorable

Anthony Tennant was keen to shake up IDV's fine wine mentality and shatter a few cultural touchstones. And who better to do this than the Cornish iconoclast Tom Jago and his South African henchman with the plumber's palate? The first place to make our mark would be an IDV international wine seminar at the Admiralty Hall in Greenwich – a wall-to-wall 'Hooray Henry' occasion.

We started by doing a bit of consumer research. A taste test was held among what were then classed as 'heavy' wine drinkers. These were people who bought at least two bottles of wine per month. In almost all markets, people classified as heavy users would account for about 80 per cent of all product sales. We decided to do a simple 'blind' taste comparison between a very good second growth Bordeaux wine and a Euro-wine called Hirondelle. The latter was a blend of Austrian, German and Hungarian red wines and it was pretty cheap. The 'blind' element meant that people didn't know what they were tasting – the wines were presented in plain glasses.

There were no videotapes in those days so I audio taped all their responses. The results were astounding, especially to the wine people. Hirondelle won hands down: it was said to be 'smoother', 'more sophisticated' and of 'higher quality' than the claret. The French wine was said to be 'corked', 'too harsh and bitter' and 'virtually undrinkable'. These were regular wine drinkers who would be the eventual arbiters of IDV's aspirations in this market. They were the voices of the future.

To say that the wine people were taken aback would have been a gross understatement. I doubt whether any one of them would have considered washing his dog in Hirondelle.

I mentioned earlier about wine bottles and labels all looking the same to the uninitiated, which was most of us, and to further develop the Admiralty Hall wind-up, I got our designer Bob Wagner to do a redesign of the Chateau Latour label to make it look 'more commercial': that is, more easily recognisable to non-Frenchmen. He used a gaudy purple background with a grotesquely large gold crown and the label carried the legend 'Full-Bodied French Red'. There were a few murmurs in the hall and a few weak chortles. Our remit was to attempt to slaughter as many sacred cows as possible, a notion not really appreciated by our audience. We were soon to put these ideas into practise. We were going to create a wine brand.

There were several wine brands out there on the market at the time and they were doing pretty good business. There was Blue Nun, a sweet white Liebfraumilch from Germany, Black Tower, also from Germany, and Mateus Rosé from Portugal. They had similar characteristics. They came in bottles that were easy to recognise on the shelf. They were widely distributed. And perhaps most importantly, they tasted good; they offered the kind of smooth, sweet, easy-drinking wine that emerging 'heavy' wine consumers were looking for. And, to really clinch the deal, they were consistent: when you bought a bottle of Blue Nun or Mateus you knew exactly what you would be getting and it would be the same again next time. These are the defining characteristics of a brand.

The question then became: how could we apply all these lessons we had learned to the development of a French wine? Wines from France still dominated the market and they represented the perceived quality

A spectacular lunch

One amusing wine moment occurred when Tom produced an empty 1928 Mouton Rothschild bottle. In a fit of mischief we decided to fill it with Lagunilla, a decent but popularly priced Rioja in the IDV stable. We grabbed a table in the very middle of their canteen at York Gate and displayed the bottle, the contents of which we drank enthusiastically with our beef casserole with chips. People would walk past our table, look at the bottle and skid to a halt, their eyes protruding like dog's balls. I never heard of any comebacks, but there must have been a chorus of disapproval somewhere in the company. "Entertaining a supplier (me) to lunch with a wine like that. Preposterous."

standard to which everyone aspired. The problem was that most modestly priced French wines didn't taste all that good to this new class of wine enthusiasts. The French paid little heed to the average consumer and especially not to the 'rosbif' English.

I was always intrigued by the notion of 'Frenchness' in respect of wines and spirits. On more than one occasion when I did focus groups on French brands in the US, if I said anything about 'the French' it was a complete turnoff. Americans regarded them as the rudest people on earth. But say that something was 'from France' and that made all the difference. That meant it had real class, was the best. It was the sophisticated choice.

The trigger for our solution came during an 'away-day' spent at a country house somewhere in Bedfordshire. The group comprised Tom, Alan Simpson and Mac Macpherson (the technical guys from Harlow), Hugh and me. These were usually general schmooze sessions where we chatted about all the business issues of the day, tossed ideas around and then sat down to lavish lunches and dinners fuelled by very good wines.

I was always the spoilsport who tried to tear these people away from deep-diving into the wine list and lunch menu to concentrate on the tasks at hand. To grab their attention I brought along some McCormick's

Wine, the final frontier: there was a marked dissonance between the wine-drinking habits and attitudes of IDV's upper class management and the emerging hordes of new wine drinkers. Our task was to change all that.

food colouring to the session and surreptitiously added it to a bottle of Blue Nun which I decanted into a green Bordeaux bottle. It looked like a red wine. I poured it out to the assembled group and asked them to taste it. No one knew what it was. They couldn't guess but concluded that it was pretty average.

Something special for the weekend
Pure gold from the house of Piat

That simple subterfuge provided the template for the creation of a new branded wine. The brief became 'could we produce a French red wine that tasted like that?' And could we create a wine that was consistent, one that would taste the same bottle after bottle? Though they didn't like my particular submission, they knew what I was after. It was a bit like our original Baileys prototype. It tasted awful but it made the point. And everyone agreed that it was worth a go. They were familiar with the background story.

Mac and his team solved the product side of the problem by introducing a new methodology into French wine-making – the addition of grape must (freshly-pressed grape juice) to sweeten the product and make it more palatable. It also provided the opportunity to make the wine more consistent by evening out the differences between batches. This was allowed in the rules and was just what we needed. A wine would now acquire the credentials of a classic brand: like a great whisky, or even a Mars bar, our wine would taste the same, time after time.

Tom was the person behind the second part of the equation, the creation of the branding. A year or two earlier, IDV had acquired a French Beaujolais company called Charles Piat and 'le Piat de Beaujolais' was their main wine. It wasn't exactly top shelf but it was a respectable middle-of-the-road French branded wine.

What really was interesting was that it had a unique bottle shape, a cross between a Perrier bottle and an Indian club. If we could jazz up the label a bit it had what we were looking for, a bottle that people would notice on the shelf and remember the next time they were out buying wine. I was pretty reticent about appropriating something that belonged to IDV's 'better wine' portfolio but Tom had no such compunction.

This time Tom was in a hurry and we summoned Bob Wagner to York Gate for a briefing on a Friday afternoon saying we wanted some first-stage designs by the following Monday. Tom had decided to call the wine 'Le Piat d'Or' so we were looking for a gold label. I suggested Benson & Hedges cigarettes as a model. That brand was in its pomp and I can remember someone telling me that while they would buy Embassy or one of the cheaper cigarette brands during the week, B&H was their cigarette of choice 'for the weekend'. It looked special in its gold box with discreet, elegant typography. That is exactly how we wanted people to view our wine – as 'something special'. Wine was nowhere near being a regular choice supermarket item in those days.

Another element that we added to the branding was the line 'Exceptionally Smooth', displayed prominently on the shoulder of the red wine bottle. The principle was simple: give diffident new wine drinkers a strong clue as to what the wine would taste like and in their own language, in this case English. And then deliver that promise in the taste.

Introduced into the UK market in 1974, Le Piat d'Or was a resounding success and became a market leader within three years. It was much quicker into its stride than Baileys because wine was (and still is) a much larger volume category than liqueurs. A bottle of wine would last an evening. A bottle of Baileys could stay around for months. It wasn't long before people unapologetically brought Le Piat d'Or to my house and it started to appear at smart ad agency and TV production company parties. And although the red variant was the lead item in our minds, a white was also created by IDV's UK company and that too was a big hit.

Le Piat d'Or spawned one of the most memorable and successful advertising campaigns ever in the drinks business in the UK based on the line 'The French Adore Le Piat d'Or', which is played back even today. I loved the ads. They were brilliantly funny and widely spoofed. But I was always a bit iffy about the headline as I doubt whether Le Piat d'Or ever crossed the Channel. (A dip into YouTube would be worthwhile as many of the old ads, serious or spoofs, are all there.)

The French clearly did not adore it and I don't think I ever met a French person who'd even heard of it. The true wine folk in IDV saw it as the devious creation of the advertising 'Anti-Christ'. I can remember one old school wine man saying that he had never drunk it and that he wouldn't even offer it to 'tradesmen'.

The French clearly did not adore it and I don't think I ever met a French person who'd even heard of it. The true wine folk in IDV saw it as the devious creation of the advertising 'Anti-Christ'. I can remember one old school wine man saying that he had never drunk it and that he wouldn't even offer it to 'tradesmen'."

Le Piat d'Or was also very successful in Japan and Canada but was kept out of the US by a Frenchman who headed the company earmarked to handle it. He did not believe in the idea of branded wine. It interfered with the natural order of things, he said. Anyway, the Americans were drinking something quite different, as you'll see from the next section...

UNE
SÉLECTION
PIAT PÈRE
& FILS

PRODUIT DE FRANCE

LE PIAT D'OR

FRENCH MEDIUM WHITE WINE

VIN DE TABLE FRANÇAIS

MIS EN BOUTEILLES PAR PIAT PÈRE & FILS, NÉGOCIANT-ÉLEVEUR
A LA CHAPELLE-DE-GUINCHAY S.-&-L.

e 75 cl   9.5% vol.

JIR 1102

UNE
SÉLECTION
PIAT PÈRE
& FILS

PRODUIT DE FRANCE

LE PIAT D'OR

FRENCH RED WINE

VIN DE TABLE FRANÇAIS

MIS EN BOUTEILLES PAR PIAT PÈRE & FILS, NÉGOCIANT-ÉLEVEUR
A LA CHAPELLE-DE-GUINCHAY S.-&-L.

e 75 cl   10.5% Vol.

1092

The gold label was inspired by
Benson & Hedges' gold cigarette
package. Name, label and
unusual bottle shape were easy to
recall when shopping for wine.

One of the UK's most memorable drink campaigns...

…Even 40 years on people recall 'The French adore' line.

Pop wine for the 'Pepsi generation'
By the time we got to Woodstock…

Wine was slowly making its way in the UK but there was a different kind of revolution taking place in the US in the late sixties. It was the time of 'Flower Power', Woodstock, free love, the Beatles, Stones, Beach Boys and Scott McKenzie's *San Francisco* – 'If you're going to San Francisco, be sure to wear some flowers in your hair'.

It was also the time of 'pop' wine. There was nothing 'flinty' about Boone Farm Apple Wine, not a trace of 'robustness' in Annie Greensprings and nobody thought of describing Zapple or Bali Hai as 'amusing' or 'presumptuous'. They were simple, fruit-flavoured 'soft drinks with balls'. They were perfect points of progression in the continuum that had started years earlier with Coke, Pepsi and 7Up.

Perhaps *Time* magazine summed up the phenomenon most pointedly: "Beyond the fact that they do not taste like real wine, pop wines have much in common: they are cheap at about $1 a bottle, and their alcohol content is a minimal 11% or so. Another advantage: they add a pleasant extra dimension to the effects of pot." Henry Luce's Republican organ promoting drinks to go with marijuana? Amazing.

There were other excitingly named members of the pop wine fraternity: Key Largo (orange, papaya and other fruit extracts), Spañada, Thunderbird, Strawberry Hill and the intriguingly named Cold Duck. The last-named was based on a traditional German recipe called Kaltes Ende, meaning 'cold end'. It was renamed Kaltes Ente, which translated more fetchingly to Cold Duck. What made it more unusual was that it was a sparkling red wine.

There were two more traditional imported wines which slotted comfortably into this accessible wine category, both of which achieved enormous volume sales in the US. These were Riuinite, a sweet sparkling red Lambrusco from Italy, and Yago, a Sangria from Spain.

Like the Brits, Americans preferred an easier initiation into wine than via challenging French offerings. Things would change, but slowly.

A few ideas that didn't make it
La Mode Americaine

Here was a wine idea that didn't work but was an interesting adventure all the same. It was the mid-1980s and varietal wines (designated by grape type – eg. Sauvignon Blanc, Cabernet Sauvignon et al) were beginning to take off. French dominance was giving way to new upstart producers like the Californians, the Australians and the Chileans – but still the French remained wedded to their 'terroire'.

Tim Ambler, who was the IDV board director in charge of innovation at the time, asked this question: "What would happen if we persuaded a Californian and a Frenchman to get together to produce French varietal wines?" Tim, being on the main board had the persuasive muscle to make that happen. How might the French respond to this idea? Would they resist it? Well that didn't happen. Even they acknowledged that the Californians knew more about varietals than almost anyone else.

We managed to find an open-minded Frenchman, Jean-Louis Camp, who was prepared to invite an American from Napa, Ed Rossi, into his winery to teach him the American way of making varietals.

Despite all predictions the collaboration was successful, the two got on extremely well and the resultant brand was called 'La Mode Americaine', a title derived from the Francois Truffaut film *La Nuit Americaine* or *Day for Night* which I had recently seen. The wines were pretty good too and Jean-Louis said that he learned a lot from Ed's New World techniques.

The wines emerged. I think the two protagonists had a great time. And the bottles, designed by Darrell Ireland, looked stunning, like serious French wines.

I think people within the company felt that the idea was too complicated for emerging consumers to understand and so, rather sadly, it was abandoned after a year's testing. But, given the huge expansion of wine sophistication 30 years on, maybe something along the lines of La Mode Americaine would be worth another shot.

Everything you wanted from a Chardonnay
But it was red

In the business of innovation, some practitioners talk glibly about 'thinking outside the box'. In my experience, many of the very best ideas have come from 'inside the box'.

One of my favourite wine ideas came from idly leafing through a document detailing the US varietal wine regulations some time in the early nineties. Well, I suppose I wasn't really 'leafing' but a boring looking document appeared on my computer so I thought I'd better wade through it. What really caught my eye was a line that said 'for bottles labelled as varietal, at least 75 per cent of the wine therein must be of that varietal'.

The language was so dry and lifeless it seemed as if they were begging you not to read it. But I persisted. My first question was what about the other 25 per cent? What could you add to a Chardonnay, for example, and still call it Chardonnay? This was at the height of the Chardonnay boom, before it was supplanted by Sauvignon Blanc.

Then I had an idea. What would happen if you added red grape skins to Chardonnay? Or if you blended in 25 per cent of a red wine like Pinot Noir? You would get red Chardonnay. Imagine someone walking along the red wine aisle in a supermarket and seeing the word Chardonnay writ large on a red wine bottle. I was in love with the thought. It all started to form in my head.

On one level it could be the red wine that you serve chilled – and we

"
What would happen if we persuaded a Californian and a Frenchman to get together to produce French varietal wines?"

Brand La Mode Americaine

Name After Truffaut's *La Nuit Americaine*

USP French wine, American style

Client Tim Ambler

Taste Fresh, fruity whites, low-tannin reds

Wine makers Ed Rossi, Jean Louis Camp

Ideal drinker Adventurers

Launched Never, no takers

Designer Darrell Ireland

The idea of a red wine described as Chardonnay would be a real show stopper on a supermarket shelf.

know that people like chilled wine. Then it could go with certain types of cheese or meatier fish such as swordfish or tuna. It could be more than just an idea for its own sake.

To bring the wine to life I commissioned a label design and displayed it in a 'magazine article'. This is a device I have used frequently over the years to show ideas in as complete a form as possible. If ideas appear as editorial rather than advertisements people give them more credibility. They will not necessarily like them for that but they will see them as genuine. The piece I produced is on page 84.

The article supposedly appeared in a magazine called *World Wine*, which was a made-up publication, and the tone of the editorial was measured rather than totally laudatory. It set out to provide the facts and let people make up their own minds about BV Red

Imagine someone walking along the red wine aisle in a supermarket and seeing the word Chardonnay writ large on a red wine bottle. I was in love with the thought."

Chardonnay. To complete the circle, I brought out my trusty bottle of McCormick's red food colouring and applied it to a well-known brand of white Chardonnay.

The idea was so intriguing that I quickly arranged some focus groups. The people I interviewed were enthusiastic enough to encourage further investigation. I then set off for Napa in California where IDV had several wineries. Could I interest the wine people in the idea? I had two visions for red Chardonnay: the first was the commercial vision. Create a red Chardonnay which, if you tasted it with your eyes closed, you would be convinced it was a white Chardonnay.

The second was the potential ego trip – for the wine makers: this would be a sophisticated blend of Chardonnay with a red wine, or with added red skins, that would win someone an award for innovation. They had the opportunity to create an entirely new varietal.

But the wine makers were only moderately interested in the idea for reasons I could not really understand. "Why do it?" seemed to be their response. Fortunately for me the US marketing people took it on and two wines were eventually produced, both based on a blend of Chardonnay and Pinot Noir. One was from Sterling Vineyards, and the other from BV (Beaulieu Vineyards). I tasted one of them – it was OK rather than outstanding and I suspect that they have both vanished from sight.

I still think red Chardonnay is a good idea. As might be white Merlot (no skins added). Maybe some adventurous young wine producer looking to offer the drinker something new and different will pick up on the idea and run with it. The Iconoclast Wine Company has a nice compelling ring to it.

Final musings
Looking for loopholes

My forays into wine country were interesting and rewarding. Le Piat d'Or was much quicker into the public consciousness than Baileys, but when we told people we'd created it they asked "What could you create? Wine is wine: did you do the label?" It wasn't so much a 'eureka moment' but a series of steps based on a combination of a bit of research and a lot of personal observation. I enjoyed the logical simplicity of it all.

Whereas Baileys was a great leap of the imagination based on past experience, wine innovation was a question of chipping away

"

On one level it could be the red wine that you serve chilled – and we know that people like chilled wine. Then it could go with certain types of cheese or meatier fish such as swordfish or tuna. It could be more than just an idea for its own sake."

Brand Sterling Chardonnay Noir

USP A red wine to be drunk ice-cold

Client None – a speculative idea

Taste Typical chardonnay with dry undertones

Ideal drinker Adventurous Chardonnay lovers

Launched Date unknown, small-scale test

Designer Unknown

RED CHARDONNAY. A NEW IDEA FROM AN INNOVATIVE WINE MAKER.

One of the most exciting innovations to arrive on the wine market in recent years is a Red Chardonnay from California.

Created by renowned wine-maker Joel Aiken, who works at Beaulieu Vineyards in Napa, it represents a totally new way of thinking about wine blending. We asked Aiken how he arrived at the idea.

"There is a tradition in wine-making of thinking 'inside the box' and blending one type of white grape or red grape with another. During our last blending season earlier in the year, we tried some new thinking. We took a popular white wine grape, Chardonnay and blended it with a small quantity of red Sangiovese grapes to see how they would bed down together. The results were quite striking. We called our wine BV RED Chardonnay. It's perfectly legal. As long as the wine contains 75% Chardonnay, it can be designated Chardonnay. Our Chardonnay just happens to be red.

It has a rich deep red colour and the first hit on the nose is the oaky buttery signature that you get with a really good Chardonnay. Then the Sangiovese kicks in, providing a roundness and depth of flavour that takes Chardonnay to another level. We were very satisfied with the marriage.

There is another bonus. Red Chardonnay is at its best served chilled, a practice that rarely works with red wines designed to be drunk at room temperature. It is a particularly good accompaniment to robust meaty fish like tuna or swordfish and is also worth trying with Stilton or other fully-flavoured cheeses."

This novel approach in a conservative sector is further testimony to the growing innovation amongst New World wine-makers. They are far more adventurous and open to new thinking than their European counterparts. It will be interesting to see how wine drinkers take to Red Chardonnay.

Kirsten Smiley

How to take a radical idea and bring it to life in an afternoon.

at things. Le Piat d'Or was an assembly of simple observations, the most fundamental of which was 'give people something they could remember next time they went off to buy a bottle'. And make sure they like the wine. Once you knew those things, the brand solution flowed logically and we got to where we wanted to be pretty quickly.

In many ways the solution was more satisfying than Baileys. I loved the idea of Red Chardonnay too because I found the inspiration in a turgid piece of government legislation about wine. It was a real thrill to see something as prosaic as 'for bottles labelled as varietal, at least 75 per cent of the wine therein must be of that varietal' give rise to such a beautifully simple idea.

As I entered the more regulated fields of whisky, vodka and gin, I would learn to appreciate the importance of tiny fragments of information such as that. I really like the way Richard Farson and Ralph Keyes put it in their book *Whoever Makes the Most Mistakes Wins*: "The best ideas aren't hidden in shadowy recesses. They're right in front of us, hidden in plain sight. Innovation seldom depends on discovering obscure or subtle elements but in seeing the obvious with fresh eyes."

I hope I managed to achieve that once in a while.

Chapter Four
Roll out the barrel

1974–early 1990s Bottle Draught 'daft' * Guinness * Guinness Light * Watney's 'Sour-Mash' Bitter * Bass LA low-alcohol bitter * Virgin Lager

One thing that struck me throughout my business life was that, no matter how many seemingly successful wine and spirit brands we developed, whenever I walked into a pub all I saw was people drinking beer. It took a long time for me to actually see someone order a Baileys, while Le Piat d'Or was far too expensive for publicans to offer as 'pouring' wine.

The great leap forward in the UK came in the seventies and eighties when warm, traditional English Bitter was overtaken by 'world beer' – cold, fizzy, bland lager. Lager even stormed one of the great bastions of traditional beer, Ireland, where Guinness was threatened by the likes of Budweiser from America and lagers from Australia, France and the rest of Europe.

Our first journey into beer was during the dark days of 1974 when Britain was working a three-day week and we were desperate to find new sources of business. But what came along was a market research project for a brewery rather than the creation of a new beer. In those days Hugh Seymour-Davies and I had an IDV retainer of £1,200 a month for our product development consultancy and little else.

The rescue came in the form of a telephone call from a man called Anthony Simonds-Gooding, an ex-colleague from my time at the advertising agency Lintas and the then marketing director of brewers Whitbread. It was on his watch that the famous 'Heineken reaches parts other beers don't reach' advertising campaign was created.

The surprise about his call was that he wanted us to tender for some research business. His company was planning a major redevelopment of their real estate assets in the City of London and wanted to go out and ask both workers and residents in the area what they thought of the idea and which facilities and services Whitbread could most usefully provide.

That was about as far removed from creating a new draught bitter or bottled lager as you could get. But times were tough and we were up for anything. Tony knew that we weren't researchers so when we asked "Why us?" he replied that he was looking for an imaginative approach to the project. He had asked several other companies to tender for the business and we were the 'wild card' in the pack.

To our utter amazement we managed to win the contract despite our answers to two key questions posed by John Archer, their serious-minded research manager: "How many of these studies have you done in the past?" And "How large is your team of interviewers?" The answers to those questions were "None," and "We don't have any interviewers".

We brought in a specialist researcher to mastermind the programme, but the real reason why we got the business was that we recommended using our 'newspaper article' idea as shown in the Red Chardonnay section in the previous chapter. We designed a half page *Financial Times* piece printed in pink with a headline that read 'XXXX Centre to open in October 1975'. The article announced plans for residential developments, restaurants, entertainment facilities and leisure services. Our aim was to find out which of these services people wanted in order to direct the development programme – and to help Whitbread make their case to the council's planning department. The article brought the whole venture to life and made it look real to those people who would be asked to assess it in our survey.

It was a tough undertaking and it took us out of our comfort zone. Drawing up quota samples from electoral registers or street maps was a long way from creating cream liqueurs. But, thanks to Heather Wild, our co-opted specialist, we delivered the research on time and within budget. Whitbread got its planning permission and the redevelopment took place in the City. I guess that many of the urban redevelopments that you can see now in the vicinity of Chiswell Street and the Whitbread offices may have started life in our pink document.

The gross value of the study was over £20,000 and we netted about £6,000 profit. That really saved our bacon in 1974. And more power to Anthony Simonds-Gooding for taking a punt on rank outsiders. He went on to head up BSB during the great satellite wars with Rupert Murdoch and Sky.

To me, English pubs in the sixties were like the beer they sold: dull, austere and down-beat. When I think back they always appear in black & white.

English beer
Culture shock

One of my earliest impressions of England when I first arrived from South Africa had come from its beer: warm, metallic and decidedly unrefreshing. It came a few hours after leaving Southampton docks in November 1961 following our disembarkation on arrival from Cape Town. We took a coach to London and stopped at a pub somewhere near Guildford for lunch and I ordered a beer. We had just had two weeks on board ship drinking ice-cold Tuborg and Amstel, bland fizzy Danish and Dutch lagers. They were much like the beer we had at home.

English cask beer was awful, I thought, on first acquaintance. It was warm, flat and full of rather sickening flavour. It would take some getting used to. By way of making our own statement in England, we took to ordering mild and bitter with occasional forays to Schmidt's in London's Charlotte Street to lash out three shillings (15p) for real fizzy German lager. It was more than double the price of English beer but well worth it.

'Daft' Guinness
Sheer genius – with a plastic syringe

The Whitbread rescue mission soon led to another approach from a brewery, this time the Guinness people from Dublin in 1974. A man called Frank Nolan telephoned and asked if he could come to see us in Greek Street. He was grey-haired, wearing a sombre dark suit and tie and had a quiet, lugubrious manner. He could have been an undertaker. He politely asked if we had a kitchen in the office – we did, after a fashion – and he disappeared for a minute before rejoining us. He asked us to talk about our work for a bit and then he drifted back into the kitchen.

He returned with a bottle of unidentified pitch-black liquid and a tall glass. He put the glass on the table, opened the bottle and poured out its contents. It looked still and black and utterly unappetising and he said nothing while he went through his sombre ritual. Hugh and I looked quizzically at each other. Hugh did quizzical very well.

Nolan then performed his coup de theatre by pulling from an inside pocket a smoky-grey plastic syringe that looked like a three-leaf clover. Without a word he placed the syringe into the glass of the still-black stuff, drew up some liquid and then squirted it back into the glass. A magical transformation then occurred. The liquid became agitated and the blackness gave way to a swirling milky chocolate brown, like a Baileys whirlpool. Then it slowly separated and settled into a perfect-looking glass of draught Guinness: deep, rich black-brown base with a tight-knit white creamy head. It was a sight to behold. I wanted to perform the ritual myself but Nolan had only brought the one bottle.

He then offered us a taste and it was remarkable. It was exactly like the real draught Guinness – the kind you got in a pub in Dublin. Frank said that they called it BDG – Bottled Draught Guinness. (We were to name it 'Daft Guinness' when work got under way because the notion of plunging this plastic thing into the beer seemed utterly ridiculous.) He wanted us to help them to take it to market.

He went on to explain the difference between the two Guinnesses that we knew: bottled and draught. It was all a matter of gas or bubbles. Bottled Guinness got its fizz from carbon-dioxide which formed large bubbles that gave the beer a bitter 'under-taste'. Exactly the same beer was used for draught Guinness, but this version was aerated with nitrogen. The nitrogen produced millions of tiny bubbles which delivered the same beer but with a much smoother creamy taste.

The company had now found a way of getting dormant nitrogen into a bottle. The plastic syringe, or 'creamer' as they called it, brought the Guinness to life by releasing the nitrogen. A friend said that if you were caught short without a 'creamer' all you had to do was take a sip of BDG, swirl it round in your mouth and then spit it vigorously back into the glass. We tried it and it worked – but it didn't seem like a particularly attractive selling platform.

The work itself was really interesting and it gave me the opportunity to use my recently acquired focus group moderator skills. We did groups among regular Irish draught Guinness drinkers in Dublin. First we outlined the idea and asked them to tell us what they thought of it; next we gave them the product to 'activate' using the creamer themselves, and then finally we let them taste it. And at the end of the groups, we gave each of them a six-pack plus creamer so that they could take BDG home to try out on their friends. They were invited back for follow-up groups. Not surprisingly, with all the free beer on offer, recruitment was not a problem and every single person came back for a second go.

The idea on first viewing was regarded suspiciously, especially the creamer element, which consumers renamed 'the plunger'. That didn't sit comfortably and people asked what would happen if they didn't have one available – or if it got dirty in their pockets.

The beer itself did pretty well. In fact, it did very well and there were calls for second and third glasses in each group. It was 'a very respectable pint' they said but could never really match up to 'the real thing'. It lacked that 'extra something' that characterised the perfect

A man's pub is his castle

One of the more interesting aspects of this development was what I saw as the social consequence of Bottled Draught Guinness. Hitherto, Guinness was the Irishman's excuse for going to the pub. It was his beer of choice and you couldn't get it at home – so he had to go out to get it. If bottled draught was as good as the company made out, his excuse for escaping to the pub would disappear. But these men did concede that BDG would enable them to extend their pub-drinking occasions by making it available at home when the pubs closed.

Our work showed that punters were interested and Bottled Draught Guinness was launched in Ireland with some excellent advertising. Headlines showing a refrigerator filled with BDG carried the line 'Open all Hours', while others said 'Head for Home' and 'My Guinness, My Goodness'. It was pretty successful and paved the way for the second generation packaged draught product in a can with the famous 'widget'. That is the major packaged draught Guinness to this day.

pint of Guinness that you got in the best pubs.

In one of the groups I decided to take the men on and offered them a challenge. I asked the barman downstairs – we were upstairs in a pub – if he could pour a fresh pint of draught Guinness in the bar. I then poured a pint of BDG. I offered the men double their £5 attendance fee or quits if they could identify which was which. To my surprise nobody would take up my offer. Perhaps the beer wasn't as 'average' as these men had suggested.

Let there be (Guinness) Light
Walking on the moon

After BDG, the Guinness people were satisfied with our work and we were then invited to have a look at a brand that was already on the market but not doing very well. It was called Guinness Light.

The origins of the idea went back to the late 1960s and the launch in America of a beer called Miller Lite. At 4% alcohol it was only marginally less alcoholic than standard US beers – but it spearheaded a new category. It was advertised on the platform of being 'less filling' than other beers and one of the keys to its success was that it was endorsed in TV commercials by retired athletes, footballers and baseball stars. (I cannot see that kind of support being allowed for an alcoholic drink today.)

In the early 1970s, sales of draught Guinness were falling away among the key 18–24 age group in Ireland. Fizzy, refreshing, undemanding lagers were taking the high ground. At that stage Guinness owned almost everything in Ireland: 90 per cent of lager and bitter and about 96 per cent of stout.

Guinness Stout was central. It was the young man's rite of passage to Irish manhood. It had to be protected. Taking a leaf out of the Miller book and riding on its success, the company decided to create Guinness Light. A lighter, less full-bodied black stout was produced which looked almost exactly like Guinness 'Heavy'. It was tested exhaustively among 18–24 year old men, their key target. The extent of the preference was extraordinary and Guinness Light looked like a sure-fire winner. We were given a truckload of research data which proved it. (As I mention elsewhere in this book, I have always been amazed at the totemic status that market research enjoys. When the 'day of judgement' came for Guinness Light, the market researchers were nowhere to be found.)

It was introduced across Ireland with great brouhaha. Every pub had it and they were festooned with Guinness Light material: show-cards, drip mats, posters and special printed glasses. TV commercials featured Neil Armstrong walking on the moon with a deep-throated American voiceover proclaiming "They said it couldn't be done" to a background of Richard Strauss's *Also Sprach Zarathustra* space anthem.

What the ad appeared to say was that the sheer technological genius associated with creating a watered-down Guinness was on a par with putting man on to the moon. It was puff-breasted hyperbole of the most blatant kind. And it was soon to be exposed by the hard-working Irish man-in-the-street.

Our task, should we wish to accept it, was to go and find out why Guinness Light wasn't setting the world on fire; why its sales were falling way below expectation. What was the noise in the marketplace? We went out and carried out focus groups among young men who had seen, heard of or tried Guinness Light. We did the research in Dublin and Galway.

Everything was perhaps best explained by a single young man we interviewed in one of our focus groups in Galway. He described his first encounter with Guinness Light: "I walked into my local bar and it was decked out with Guinness Light material. It was everywhere: posters, and beer mats. There were even special Guinness Light pint glasses. It all struck a chord. I remembered seeing a TV advert for it and I decided to order a pint. It appeared in its special glass and looked pretty tasty. But as I put it to my lips a hand tapped me gently on the shoulder and a man said "You're cheating. You're drinking lady's Guinness".

That statement epitomised the problem. In Ireland especially, drinking is a social experience and then, more than now, pubs were broad churches, frequented by people of all ages and backgrounds. While the taste of Guinness Light may have been significantly more acceptable to young lager drinkers than regular Guinness, the idea of openly associating yourself with a weaker imitation of the real thing was an invitation to ribald comment. Guinness Light might just as well have been coloured fluorescent pink. It was not so much a case of what you liked. It was how other people regarded you.

Despite the huge research spend, the company underestimated the impact of the public house environment. They did no research among potential detractors: older draught Guinness die-hards.

The name was wrong too. Guinness Light told too much of a story about the beer and the person who was drinking it. A more nondescript, less propositional name like Guinness 'Special' would have represented a far more acceptable badge for the young drinker to wear. But who wanted openly to advertise that they couldn't manage 'the real thing'? Not in the 1970s and not in Ireland.

The other key mistake that Guinness made was to over-hype the new Light. One older respondent talking in a focus group piped up: "Well, they said it couldn't be done and they were right. It couldn't." There was a kind of smug, self-righteous pleasure in seeing the mighty Guinness being unceremoniously brought down to earth.

There was little we could do except tell Guinness what we had heard. We did make some suggestions, but the damage had already been done. One idea we put up was they should withdraw their TV campaign and switch to radio spots – cheaper and easier to produce. They should focus on Guinness Light's functional attribute: that it was the refreshing face of Guinness. I recalled reading that coal miners in Wales and the North-East of England drank lighter, lower-strength beers, but in huge quantities, to restore them after arduous hours underground. There was a justification for a lighter Guinness.

But it was all too little, too late. Guinness Light was a massive failure and the number of people who would have been prepared to admit that it was their idea would have rattled around on the back seat of a Reliant Robin (which is a small, three-wheeled British car).

The two Guinness projects provided a whole new slant on our development as consultants. We were inputting to other people's ideas rather than being asked to create something new. In the case of BDG, we helped bring a pretty revolutionary idea to market. And Guinness Light was a 'hindsight' job, and as everyone knows, hindsight is always 20-20. I was still keen to put a beer brand into my portfolio.

Refreshing Guinness Light. A totally new beer.

There's never been anything like it. New Guinness Light. Cool. Refreshing. Satisfying. And a lot lighter than it looks.

GUINNESS *Light*

What one small step did for mankind we've done for beer.

Guinness Light: from the sublime to the not-so-sublime.

Watney's Red Revolution
Better dead than red

IDV had a sister company within the Grand Metropolitan group, a brewer called Watneys. I was invited in by another consultancy company to help it develop a new bitter beer for Watneys. The prospect was an exciting one although I have already chronicled my dislike of English bitter. So it would be a huge challenge.

Like Guinness Light, Watneys too had been dogged by high-profile failure. In the sixties it had launched Watneys Red in an attempt to apply 'detergent marketing' techniques to the launch of a beer. This would be modern marketing brought to bear in an antiquated, unsophisticated market sector. In those days in the UK people referred to management in breweries as 'the Beerage', posh authoritarian types whose ideas were a century out of date. So the introduction of smart young marketing hot-shots was a real culture shock to the industry. But Watneys had discovered marketing and wanted beer to become a brand. The new age had begun.

It was all summed up by a member of the Watneys marketing management who stated "I want people to be able to go into any Watneys pub, from Land's End to John O'Groats, and be able to get exactly the same food and exactly the same beer in pubs with exactly the same décor". This was how Watneys Red would be transformed into a brand, to sail under the banner of the 'Watneys Red Revolution'.

As an article in the *Financial Times* stated, "Watneys... was the most reviled brand of all. Many drinkers hated not only its taste but the marketing that accompanied it, from irritating advertising jingles to entire pub refits. In 1971, in a misguided search for radical chic, Watneys mounted a campaign which urged beer-drinkers to 'Join the Red Revolution'. Pubs were painted corporate red, bar staff wore red socks and posters featured look-alikes of Chairman Mao, Nikita

Khrushchev and Fidel Castro supping Watneys".

Another piece, in the *Northampton Echo*, went on to say, "Then the real thing... or more precisely, Watney's Red, probably the weakest and least beer-like chemical concoction known to man".

People didn't want all pubs to be the same – they wanted them to be local and individual. These were pubs, not hamburger bars or coffee shops. They wanted the beer to vary, depending on the competence of the local landlord. And they claimed they wanted real beer, not the artificial keg stuff. Watneys Red became known as 'love-in-a punt'. (Love-in-a-punt is British slang for weak or watered down beer and I will leave it to the reader to work out why...)

So here I was, in 1985, 15 years on, looking for an idea for a new beer for the Watneys company. Although Red and the Watneys brand name had been dead for years, the legend persisted. Even young drinkers who were infants during the Red Revolution debacle seemed to be aware of the brand's reputation. The punt sailed on.

By this time I was working on my own and commissioned by co-consultants who were my only link to the Watneys people. In fact, the first time I met the actual client was when I presented my proposals. It was not the most enthralling atmosphere for coming up with a great new idea. Watneys via a slightly roundabout route requisitioned the development of a new bitter beer. It was a daunting prospect.

I stumbled across the beginnings of an answer to this brief in, of all places, a car magazine. It was an article on the Czech car, Skoda. Back then, certainly to people in the UK, Skoda could be called the Watney's Red of the automobile industry. Here was a brand that aroused strong emotions, invariably negative ones. This was the kernel of my idea.

I was formulating a theory. There were brands that most people thought were OK: not special, not brilliant, just ordinary. And those were in the majority. Then there were brands that people loved. But I had real difficulty working out which ones generated real passion and enthusiasm. Perhaps today Apple would fall into that category. And Virgin in the 1990s. And then there were brands which people actively loathed: Marmite, Guinness Light and Watneys Red. Those were the brands that people made jokes about.

And that became my theory: let's start with something that people really don't like. That's a strong emotion. Let's then build it up to make it likeable, maybe even respectable. Let's broadcast that the new beer comes from Watneys and give people a chance to forgive and forget. I was excited by this insight. But it would take a brave client to buy it.

Watneys Sour Mash Bitter
So challenging, I have to try it

To achieve this we had to start with the beer itself. It had to be a keg beer because that was where the market was going. But it also had to be excellent, the best that the Watneys brewers could deliver. I even suggested that we should present it 'blind' to the CAMRA people (the Campaign for Real Ale which was, and still is, the arbiter of English bitter beer quality) and get them to provide their imprimatur. Let them judge the beer on its taste and not its provenance. And it must receive their unreserved approval as the finest beer of its kind. It must be good enough for their plaudits.

We must also make the product sound different, like a genuinely new beer. In liaison with a brewer friend I discovered that we could apply the term 'sour-mash' to this product – it was all to do with the level of acidity in the mash that produced the beer. This appropriated a term used by very fashionable American whiskey brands such as Jim Beam and Jack Daniel's which were growing in popularity in the UK.

Watneys 'Sour-Mash' Bitter had a real contemporary ring to it at the time. I thought that the idea of sour-mash beer would encourage trial. It suggested something new, different, even challenging – and it wasn't the usual clichéd laudatory hype that was often associated with new products. Watneys needed to tread carefully – and modestly.

I loved the notion of bringing
Watneys back from the
dead. 'Sour-mash bitter'
had a real ring to it.

Taste test
Watneys 'Sour-Mash' Bitter

I did some focus groups among young men who were all aware of the Watneys Red myth. For them the legend of love-in-a-punt definitely lived on. Watneys 'Sour-Mash' bitter was not an immediately inviting prospect. But when they thought about it and tasted the beer – we used a very good 'off-the-peg' premium bitter to exemplify the idea – their views began to change. They thought the beer itself was fine and there was some interest in the notion of giving Watneys a second chance.

As one man said, "They'll try harder this time". And 'Sour-Mash' bitter had a daredevil ring to it. "The combination of Watneys and Sour-Mash sounds like a real turn-off. I may just have to try it." Looking back, their views may well have reflected those of, say, present-day Skoda buyers. In the beginning, Skoda was a 'joke' automobile, viewed in England and America as being similar to Lada or Trabant. After its acquisition by Volkswagen, Skoda turned the corner and now offers well-engineered, attractive automobiles. Today the Skoda is a serious car and all is forgiven. People are proud to own one. I was after that sentiment with Watneys 'Sour-Mash' bitter.

I thought of the UK tabloid press getting hold of our idea for a new Watneys bitter. The Red Revolution debacle would be played back in the papers and on TV. They'd be all over it like a rash. But if the beer itself was as good as I wanted it to be, as it had to be, anything would be possible. We could use all that negative publicity to our advantage.

There was an unfortunate punch-line to this story. Where it really mattered, the idea sank, like a stone. I did the presentation with a delightful man called Brian Palmer. He was the middle man in this relationship. He had been famous in another life as the man who wrote the very first commercial to appear on UK television, for Gibbs SR toothpaste – "Tingling Fresh SR" was the message.

We showed up at Watneys for a 2 o'clock meeting. Our client, who I had never met, didn't show until nearly 5. He'd been at a lunch. He instantly hated the idea of Watneys 'Sour-Mash' Bitter. In fact the notion of using the Watneys name at all induced a quiet fury. The meeting lasted about 10 minutes. Next morning Brian called to tell me that I had been summarily fired. I should never darken their doors again.

Bass Low-Alcohol Bitter
A beer brand at last – up to a point

One market that seems to have come and gone is low-alcohol beer. It was a real growth category in the early 1980s and there were heavily advertised beers like Barbican, Kaliber and Clausthaler. In 1984, Whitbread introduced the first low-alcohol bitter beer, White Label, and an opportunity presented itself.

There had been a great advertising agency shake-out in the 1980s and one of my closest friends, Gordon Canning, found himself without a job. We had lunch one day and he asked if we could work together. He would go out and hustle for clients and I would create the new ideas. It seemed like a good plan to me, as he was a very good friend and hustling for business wasn't my strong suit. And by this time Hugh and I had split up, so I needed some company.

Gordon didn't take long to find us a client: the Midlands brewers Bass. It wanted to develop a low alcohol (1%) bitter beer to compete with newly arrived Whitbread's White Label. Gordon had persuaded the client that we were the people for the job.

Perhaps the first thought that we had was that one of the intrinsic advantages of bitter over lager beer was that it had more flavour. A low-alcohol bitter beer could use its stronger, more pronounced taste to compensate for the absence of alcohol. Looking for a logical, functional way in to this problem was right up my alley.

Now, this wasn't rocket science. The solution came during a half-hour chat looking at the White Label product and tasting the beer. The packaging, a can, looked light and un-beer like. First impressions were that it looked like weak beer with its white background and red and green colour scheme. It seemed like a very flimsy idea.

This weak persona then carried through to the beer itself which was pale and lager-like in colour and with no discernible taste. It did not take advantage of the flavour opportunity that was presented by being a bitter rather than lager.

Full, satisfying flavour would compensate…
…for low alcohol

We started by talking to the Bass brewing team. We asked them if they could develop a really full-flavoured 1% bitter where the strong, satisfying taste would go some way towards compensating for the lower level of alcohol. They said it could be done. We also wanted a beer which was darker and richer-looking in colour than White Label or any of the lager brands. It must look like the full-bodied, satisfying bitter that we wanted it to be.

Our next step was the packaging. We wanted a bottle rather than a can because it fitted the more traditional character of bitter beer and would present our beer as a serious, authentic product. We also wanted to use dark colours on the labelling to reinforce the idea of a rich, satisfying product – and to use words like 'full-bodied' on the label to communicate the taste characteristics of the beer itself. Remember Le Piat d'Or and 'Exceptionally Smooth'. The same principle was applied here, and indeed to many brands I developed later.

So here we were. All dressed up and ready to go. We had a bottle and label and we had set up focus groups in Sutton Coldfield near

"

A low-alcohol bitter beer could use its stronger, more pronounced taste to compensate for the absence of alcohol."

Brand Bass LA

USP Low-alcohol beer bursting with flavour

Client Bob Littler, Bass Brewing

Taste Rich, nutty bitter beer

Ideal drinker Real beer lovers needing a rest

Launch 1987

Designer Gerry Barney, Sedley Place

Birmingham in the heart of Bass territory. We were going to test our beer, Bass LA (low-alcohol), against Whitbread White Label to see how our idea would play out.

Then disaster struck. The brewing team called two days before the research and said there was 'trouble at mill' and there would be no beer for us. We were committed to doing the research, so what could we do?

I went back to my Baileys days and launched into D-I-Y product-development mode. We went out to a store and bought two dozen cans and bottles of bitter beers. We also bought some Kaliber, a no-alcohol

I went back to my Baileys days and launched into D-I-Y product-development mode. We went out to a store and bought two dozen cans and bottles of bitter beers. We also bought some Kaliber, a no-alcohol lager that we might use as our base product. And finally I got in touch with my friends at IDV and scrounged some caramel colouring."

lager that we might use as our base product. And finally I got in touch with my friends at IDV and scrounged some caramel colouring.

After an hour spent sampling all the bitters on show, we concluded that the best candidate by far would be Ruddles County, so that became our flavour agent for Bass LA. Our formula was three parts Kaliber at 0% alcohol, one part Ruddles at 4%, which brought the overall proof down to 1%. We then added caramel colouring to deliver a rich, full-bodied looking bitter beer. It tasted really good and delivered our original idea pretty well. We were ready to roll.

We did six focus groups across three evenings with eight people per group. We started each group with a blind taste-comparison between Whitbread White Label and Bass LA. Of the 48 tastings we carried out, 45 preferred our home-made Bass LA. It was a landslide. Our product looked better in the glass and clearly tasted better. And the reasons people gave for their preferences were heart-warming in the extreme: 'better/fuller flavour', 'more satisfying' and 'more like a real bitter'. And, by the way, when we did the 'blind' tasting, we made no mention of low-alcohol beer.

We were delighted with the success of our product and were able to use it to provide a very clear brief to the brewing team. And their eventual interpretation worked out very well too. The final product had a full, satisfying flavour and was well received by drinkers looking to cut down on alcohol intake.

The 'formula' worked: if you take out the alcohol, compensate with flavour. But the brand didn't. Launched in the mid-1980s, Bass LA was around for a while but vanished quietly a few years later. It was probably the wrong time for these products as none of the other players are much in evidence now. Whatever happened to Barbican, Kaliber and Clausthaler? The products were probably not good enough. Any beer is a kind of relationship: you drink a lot of it and you drink it often. Under these trying conditions, the product has to be exceptional.

There had been heated discussions about the sub-name 'LA'. To me it meant 'Bass Bitter but weaker', like Guinness Light. That immediately set up the expectation of a 'distress purchase'. I would have preferred a name that implied a 'different kind of Bass bitter' or something nondescript like Bass XL. The client had his way. I always thought that a dark stout like Guinness would translate well into a low-alcohol variant. But the toxic fallout from Guinness Light will probably take another 50 years to dissipate.

Virgin enters the beer market

Following successful moves into cola, energy drinks and vodka, Richard Branson's Virgin Company has recently moved into beer with the introduction of Virgin Lager. Their new product is available now in selected outlets and they are planning national distribution in the summer.

We recently interviewed Richard Branson on his new move and he had this to say:

"As an expanding and innovative company, Virgin Trading continually looks at markets where consumers are offered little by way of quality and real choice. As we did with cola, our Virgin Lager is intended to shake up the highly competitive UK lager market. We will be offering a British lager to compete with the growing number of American and European lagers that are invading our market. We will be offering a top quality product that really tastes better than the competition."

In keeping with other Virgin products, Virgin lager has been developed to offer the consumer something unique. Brewed in the North East of England, the beer combines the best quality whole hops – not powders or extracts as used by many other lagers – and the purest available spring water. Our taste panels have sampled the beer and find it very clean-tasting and refreshing with no bitter after-taste.

We were shown a recent research report where Virgin lager was tested against a group of leading brands on sale in the UK. The evidence showed the Virgin product ahead of the field : good enough to satisfy Branson's tough criteria.

We shall be monitoring its progress with interest. *Jim Forres*

How the idea of Virgin lager was first floated.

Virgin territory
Vodka, cola, lager?

In the early 1990s I was introduced to the Midlands brewer, Wolverhampton & Dudley, makers of the famous Banks's Bitter, and through it became involved with Sir Richard Branson and the Virgin brand. It was the era of Virgin vodka and Virgin cola and he had decided that an 'unholy' trinity should be completed with Virgin lager.

I was asked to research the idea and feed my recommendations back to Branson. This was a very exciting prospect as he was probably the most charismatic businessman in the country and the chance to work for him was incredibly exciting.

I toured the country talking to young lager drinkers. Branson and Virgin were huge hits with these men. They saw him as 'one of us' and if he brought a lager to market, it would be well worth a try.

But I had a nagging feeling about the idea. I have always been a product man, suspicious of the notion of 'the brand über alles'. If you can give people a rational, functional reason for buying a product, do it. It helps. By this time Branson's assaults on the cola and vodka markets were beginning to flag. They offered no tangible reason to choose them over Coke or Smirnoff and Virgin seemed to be going into everything.

When I eventually met Branson at his London house in Holland Park, us in suits and Richard and team in jeans, it all became clearer. He wanted his beer to be a Budweiser 'taste-alike' but I felt that to really work it needed to be differentiated, like his airline. The Virgin brand should stand for more than just another cola, vodka or indeed lager. It seemed to me to be the foundation stone of his business empire. Being Virgin, to me, must mean being better.

Perhaps fortunately for all, the Virgin Lager brand never surfaced. Sir Richard probably took on board the lessons learned with failed cola and vodka. Virgin could do better than that – and frequently did.

Chapter Five
Softly does it

1984–1990 Dexters Sports drink * Aqua
Libra * Purdey's * Pfaffs and others

There was a prescient view in the early 1980s that the drinks business would come under attack from various sources in the years to come. There would be the health lobby that saw increasing levels of alcohol intake putting drinkers' health in peril. There was growing concern about drinking and driving. And the social impact of alcohol abuse was becoming a major issue. But then again there were governments who would be looking for increasing levels of revenue from alcoholic drink producers. Alcohol was a good earner.

Innovation in IDV had been taken over by Tim Ambler, a board director and probably the most inspiring client I ever served. Tom Jago, who had been our prime contact at IDV from 1969 to 1983, had left to join Moet Hennessy, the champagne and cognac house, and Mac Macpherson, the chemist who had created the Baileys product, had taken over his position at head office. Tim was the board director to whom we both reported.

Ambler's vision was simple enough to express – but extremely difficult to execute. What he required was 'a range of added-value non-alcoholic drinks that would provide the consumer with a whole new slant on soft drinks' – and would allow the company to command a premium price. After all, simple fizzy water like Perrier had taken the world by storm and was charging more than decent bottled beer so that if we could enhance our products sufficiently, we could at least enter their league.

We had a blank piece of paper with a short, simple wish list and the issue was where on earth do we start?

Catching the wave
If Perrier can charge a premium for fizzy water...

The only clue we had was that we were looking for products with healthy overtones, possibly connected with sport and leisure. And given that quite a few of the team were participants in various sports, we decided to start there. But we still didn't quite know what to look for and in a moment of desperation, we decided to carry out some focus groups. Let's talk to consumers, throw out a few half-formed ideas and see what happens.

We headed south for Croydon, a suburb on the outskirts of London, and talked to young men, young women and older people with families, in an attempt to fit things together. We also managed to get hold of a few sports drinks that were on sale in the UK. There was Gatorade from the US, Isostar from Germany and the strangely named Pocari Sweat from Japan – surely something was lost in translation with that one.

There was very little knowledge of these drinks among our groups and each of them attracted quite a lot of interest. But they seemed a little too 'specialist' for ordinary folk. While a few of the younger men saw their physical pursuits as competitive activities, most people took part in exercise to lose weight, stay in trim or maintain a general level of healthiness. Competition had nothing to do with their regimes.

Another thing we noticed during the day's interviewing was that, while the products under review provided nutrients to boost energy and therefore performance, they were also extremely high in calories. This sparked off an idea which I jotted down between the third and fourth groups. It was something that seemed to pop out after talking to these Croydon people. The line I wrote was 'Dexters puts back the minerals that exercise takes out – without the calories.'

I introduced the idea by suggesting that I had read about it in a magazine recently. Viewed alongside the likes of Gatorade and

Pocari Sweat, people thought it sounded 'sensible' and they might be interested in trying it. It was hardly an overwhelming endorsement but at least it provided an opening to what had been a difficult challenge.

That became the template for the first brand in what would emerge as a range of new non-alcoholic drinks. We took the idea to Tim Ambler – I was never sure what he was expecting – and to our surprise and delight he bought it as it stood. On the outside it would be a sports drink but its 'firm underbelly' would be its very low calorie content, perfect for people who wanted to stay in shape.

We would take the best that Gatorade and Pocari Sweat had to offer and shape it to fit the needs of ordinary health-conscious people. The technical team even co-opted the assistance of a Dr Ron Maughan, an international authority on sports nutrition, to ensure that the basis for the product was founded on technical evidence. We were intent on making our product as efficacious and as effective as we could. And we even stuck with the Dexters name which I really liked. It sounded macho and sporty.

Our friends from the design agency Sedley Place came up with a brilliant theme for the can. They used a motif that looked like the tread from a high-tech running shoe. The early 1980s was the beginning of the trainer revolution with the likes of Nike, Adidas and Reebok cutting a huge swathe through fashion-conscious, health-aware UK youth.

Tim had decided that if this operation was to be successful we needed a full-time person running it and appointed a woman, Claire Watson, to head up the team. Between them they came up with the devastatingly simple sales strategy which said: "Let's focus the sale of these products on outlets where people will buy them." No point in putting Dexters into supermarkets. Unless millions was spent on advertising, nobody would know what it was.

Instead, they decided to seed these products where they would have the best chance of success and in line with Marshal McLuhan's theory, the medium could become part of the message. Dexters was a healthy sports drink because it was seen and sold in sports and health clubs. This was to become the strategy for all the products in this range. 'Where you sold' was a key component in 'What you were'.

"
Dexters puts back the minerals that exercise takes out – without the calories."

Brand Dexters Isotonic

USP Turns slimmers into sportsmen

Client Tim Ambler

Taste Sharp, sparkling passion fruit

Launch 1985

Designer Bob Celiz, Sedley Place

One of the aspects of Dexters that I really liked was that it was a no-calorie drink that someone who was conscious about their weight could order in a public place with impunity. Walk into a pub and loudly call for a 'Diet Coke' and you were broadcasting the fact that you were fat. Ask for a Dexters and you were announcing that you were a bit of a sportsman.

Aqua Libra
Fit for a princess

Dexters was up and running but Tim wouldn't allow us to rest on our laurels. He wanted a second drink which he code-named Claire II in honour of Claire Watson. Although it took quite a few months to develop, Dexters was pretty easy once we knew where we were going. The big issue was how we followed it. What kind of idea would be a fitting companion to a low-calorie sports drink?

If we were to create a range of products, there needed to be some consistent message which would connect all the individual brands. (As it was to turn out, Dexters, despite being the first brand in the range, became the 'odd man out' and we were later to move off in a different direction. Dexters remained in the range but was less of a neat fit with the 'positive health' idea that was to emerge.)

This became 'innovation by a hundred curries'. Well, not quite. Claire II became harder and harder to crack and we would meet with Tim on Wednesday nights over a curry and throw ideas around. Nothing emerged. Tim tried to be helpful and on one occasion said something like: "How about this? There's this very smart Soho bash. Every single top model in town is in attendance, I am standing in the midst of them, and we are all drinking Claire II. What will it be? That should make it easy for you." The hell it did. We still hadn't a clue as to where to begin. But Claire II did come to life quite unexpectedly and it was to provide the basis for the plan for the other products in the range.

By this time work was going quite well and I had acquired a colleague to work with me, a very bright woman called Annabel Allott. She had become embroiled in the quest for Claire II and, like the good professional she was, she started reading books on health. One such book was called *The Joy of Beauty*, written by one of the gurus of the time – and still a power in the field – Leslie Kenton. Being interested in jazz I was impressed that she was the daughter of the famous Stan Kenton, a pianist and big band leader, whom I recalled from the 1950s.

I was in the office on a call to the Gas Board and idly leafing through the book, waiting to make my connection. I can't remember whether they had muzak then. I chanced upon a chapter headed 'alkaline balance' and that really captured my attention. It postulated that our western diet was made up largely of foods which created 'acid ash' in the bloodstream. What we needed was a product that created 'alkaline ash' to establish the essential balance that would enable healthy living. In Eastern diets these alkaline-forming ingredients abounded.

I really became excited and, as I dug deeper, I discovered a whole host of ingredients that would promote alkaline balance – ingredients like sunflower and sesame seeds, certain fruit juices, vitamins and nutrients. "This is it!" I thought and proceeded to write out a short proposal to present to Tim Ambler. I telephoned his office and, fortunately, he was in the UK and agreed to see me in a couple of hours. This was a member of the main board of a large global company. I was pretty surprised.

A good idea is one where the buyer and seller are on exactly the same wavelength. I outlined the idea to Tim in about two minutes. He saw exactly what I was on about and he bought the idea immediately. "Let's do it" he said and from that moment the rest of the development didn't take too long.

First, there was the brand name. Annabel and I had space in the offices of the design company, Sedley Place. In my case, when the adrenalin was flowing I would involve anyone willing to listen in a new idea. I burst into reception and asked the woman running the desk, Agnes Stanley, "What's another word for balance?" She thought for a moment and said "How about Libra?" That was it. "We'll call the product Aqua Libra". We'd been groping in the dark for about six months and here, in a nano-second, the whole idea came together. Agnes didn't know what hit her but was pretty excited at being able to make a significant contribution to the birth of a new brand.

The next thing we needed was what we called a 'concept board'. Basically it was a hand-drawn picture of the bottle, brand name and all, which would bring Aqua Libra to life. The Sedley team were pretty

Princess Diana, the 'People's Princess', selected Aqua Libra alongside champagne as favourite drinks in a CV feature in *You* magazine in *The Mail on Sunday*. At that time could there ever have been a better endorsement?"

busy and I telephoned Bob Wagner, the man who had designed the Baileys pack. I asked him to use a 75cl bottle, the size of a wine bottle, and wanted a design that looked distinctive and natural, like a traditional herbal remedy.

I think that during our chat on the telephone words like 'weighing scales' and 'waterfalls' were covered. Bob was required to deliver the design within four days so that Tim could present it to the IDV board.

Mac Macpherson and I went off on a business trip to New York and returned on the day of Tim's meeting. We got to the office at about 7am and there on Mac's desk was Bob Wagner's board. We opened the parcel and inspected Bob's work. It was perfect. He had brought Aqua Libra to life on a piece of white board. It was magical. I could see Tim and his Supermodels in a smart club, all drinking Aqua Libra. We had a brand.

SPARKLING

AQUALIBRA

HERBAL FRUIT JUICE DRINK

INGREDIENTS:
SPARKLING SPRING WATER, PASSION
FRUIT JUICE, GRAPE & APPLE JUICES
(FROM CONCENTRATES), NATURAL
FLAVOURINGS & EXTRACTS: MELON,
SESAME, SUNFLOWER, TARRAGON,
ANGELICA ROOT, CORIANDER
SEED, ELDERFLOWER &
SIBERIAN GINSENG.

BASED ON A SWISS RECIPE FOR
CALLITHEKE UK LIMITED,
1 YORK GATE LONDON NW1

DRY

e 75cl

FD1/1

HELPS RESTORE ALKALINE BALANCE

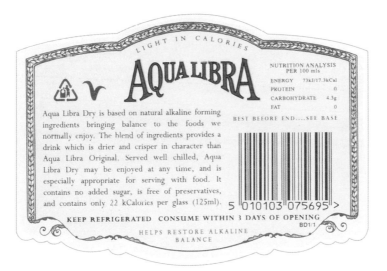

LIGHT IN CALORIES

AQUALIBRA

Aqua Libra Dry is based on natural alkaline forming
ingredients bringing balance to the foods we
normally enjoy. The blend of ingredients provides a
drink which is drier and crisper in character than
Aqua Libra Original. Served well chilled, Aqua
Libra Dry may be enjoyed at any time, and is
especially appropriate for serving with food. It
contains no added sugar, is free of preservatives,
and contains only 22 kCalories per glass (125ml).

NUTRITION ANALYSIS
PER 100 mls

ENERGY   73kJ/17.3kCal
PROTEIN   0
CARBOHYDRATE   4.3g
FAT   0

BEST BEFORE END....SEE BASE

5 010103 075695 >

KEEP REFRIGERATED CONSUME WITHIN 3 DAYS OF OPENING
BD1/1
HELPS RESTORE ALKALINE
BALANCE

Another 'hole in one' from Bob Wagner after a short telephone briefing.

One of the great things about working with people who are high up in an organisation is that their 'fear of failure quotient' will be pretty low, if it exists at all. In discussing Aqua Libra with Tim he agreed that it would be pointless trying to do any market research on the idea. The notion of 'alkaline balance' with all its attendant mystery and strange ingredients would never survive a focus group.

In the words of one of Nike's most famous straplines, we decided to 'Just do it'. Crucially, Claire Watson and everyone else in the team were 100 per cent behind the idea too. Bob's design magically gave Aqua Libra instant appeal. It was utterly compelling.

Aqua Libra was to become one of the iconic drinks of the 1980s and top models did indeed order it publicly and often. I suppose the ultimate expression of Tim's 'top model' objective came when none other than Princess Diana, the 'People's Princess', selected Aqua Libra alongside champagne as favourite drinks in a CV feature in *You Magazine* in the *Mail on Sunday*. Could there ever have been a better endorsement? She was the 'top model' sans pareil. And it was a spontaneous choice with no PR money changing hands.

My own ad campaign
At last

One of the problem areas with Aqua Libra was coming up with advertising for a brand that was showing real momentum. Try as they did, the agency's creative team couldn't deliver. Much to my surprise, and delight, I rescued the situation by writing the 'CV' campaign, inspired by the Princess of Wales piece in the *Mail on Sunday*. The ads, which ran in the smart colour supplements, set out to communicate the idea of 'balance' by showing attractive people with balanced interests. The advertisements only ran for a few weeks with modest expenditure, but it was terrific to have a campaign out there at last.

Love it or hate it
Not as Swiss as it seemed

One of the best things about Aqua Libra was the product itself. It was complex, interesting and tended to polarise opinion. Some people loved it and others hated it. I can remember an article written by the journalist Craig Brown where he described Aqua Libra as tasting like 'liquid lipstick'. He clearly wasn't a fan. I think the beauty of Aqua Libra was that the flavour took some acquiring. It was a drink with an adult taste. It was a great exemplar of the superb product development group in IDV. And it took real courage for the management to go with something that might not be universally acceptable.

However, there had been one small fly in the Aqua Libra ointment. The brand had become big news and Claire Watson and I were approached by Matthew Norman from the *Mail on Sunday*. He wanted to write a piece on Aqua Libra and she and I were thought to be the best available representatives to discuss it with him.

One of the early areas of debate during the development of the brand was that Tim Ambler had suggested that we include the line 'Made from a special Swiss Recipe' on the bottle. He thought it would sound good and 'verify' the brand. I was dead against it because it was a complete fiction. We had a very cordial interview with Norman but after I left he started grilling Claire about the Swiss Recipe. Could he have sight of it? Where was it? I was delighted to have missed this interchange. I gathered later from Claire that he had almost attempted to storm her office.

Several weeks passed before the interview appeared and I had almost given up on it not being a regular *Mail on Sunday* reader. My introduction to it came during a cricket match one Sunday afternoon. I came out to bat and one of the opposition drew the article from his pocket and showed it to me. I was so startled and embarrassed that I was immediately dismissed. As it happened, I came out of the article quite well but the Swiss Recipe didn't get a very good press.

AQUA LIBRA

Name
Harry Burton

Birthday
30 January 196
– Aquarius

Job
Actor

Fortunes of War
Gentlemen & Players
Tears in the Rain

Music
Bob Marley & the Wailers
George Gershwin
Luther Vandross

Eating out
English Garden
(when I'm working)
Marine Ices
Cafe Fish

Clothes
Woodhouse
Notting Hill Housing Trus
Agnès B

Pet hates
Overcooked veg.
Catches dropped off
my bowling
Marbled jeans

Things I'd like to ov
A house big enough
a snooker table
366 pairs of shoes
David Byrne's suit
'Stop Making Sens

My perfect wee
A 48-hour poke

Drinks
Jack Daniels
Aqua Libra
Czechoslova
Budweiser

Personal gossip, even if you didn't know the people, could be irresistible.

Purdey's
More rhythm, less blues – or should it be fewer?

Aqua Libra was fast becoming the jewel in the crown and would provide the basis upon which all future drinks in this range would be founded. We had stumbled upon the notion of what we called 'positive health'. There had been major growth in what were termed healthy products but they were based on 'health by omission'. These products were low in calories or cholesterol or fat or sugar or alcohol or tar or nicotine or caffeine, take your pick. They had less of whatever noxious ingredient their category of products was said to contain. And by consuming them you might live longer, look better or feel better. Well, you know what I mean.

Our approach to Aqua Libra and its companion products was that they would provide health by commission or addition. We would aim to provide combinations of vitamins and other natural, health-giving ingredients to enable you to feel better, get fitter and look more beautiful. We were moving onto the edge of pharmaceuticals.

The next product, unimaginatively code-named Claire III, started from a slightly different point. I am not sure where the brief originated but we decided to aim at 'getting into the music/entertainment/film business'. Our newest version of Tim's 'top models' objective was Abbey Road Studios. Let's aim to deliver our very first case of Claire III to the music studio that was immortalised by The Beatles.

If you start with music and entertainment perhaps the first word you think of is energy. These are up-tempo activities in high-energy environments. But how can you deliver energy without caffeine or sugar or both? And the law said if you used the term energy you had to back it up with high sugar. But we were in the business of positive health. Sugar and caffeine were not part of our new remit.

The answer came from a well-used source for brand development:

Roget's Thesaurus. If you are at a loss for an idea then look for a word. Much of my business life has been about looking for words. I found it. The word was 'vitality'. It was a far looser proposition than energy and more to do with general well-being and alertness than the harsh equation of percentage kilojoules of sugar and real physical energy which the law demanded. It was also a new word. Energy was playing out. It was everywhere from Mars bars to Lucozade.

Once we had the word we did some further digging to look for vitamins and natural herbal ingredients that would help to deliver the word. Vitality. A trawl through *Culpeper's Complete Herbal* (Nicholas Culpeper was a 17th century English botanist, herbalist, physician, and astrologer) unearthed the likes of bayberry bark extract, damiana, prickly ash bark and some B vitamins to produce the base for a recipe which IDV's technical group wove into another brilliant liquid. It was perhaps not as complex and difficult as Aqua Libra, but it was pretty close. It was, as it was intended to be, another 'grown-up' drink with a flavour that might not be to everyone's taste.

With Aqua Libra the name came first and everything stemmed from that. It was a great name which everybody liked. This time the name sat across a table in a meeting. He was a bearded technical guy called Colin Purdey, very professorial, very bright and a real boffin. I am not sure he fitted the 'vitality' archetype, but a bottle of Purdey's sounded like a great call. Colin, not completely sold on the idea, learned to live with it.

Howard Waller, the graphic designer who Tom called 'the mudjik', was on the case and came up with a brilliant design. He took a wide-mouth Ruddles County beer bottle and coloured it a kind of gunmetal

The Mudjik

Howard Waller was a brilliant, volatile designer, and a man Tom Jago often referred to as 'the Mudjik' because of his black curly hair and menacing bushy eyebrows. He was constantly looking to shock and surprise, and his work always stood out.

silver with graphics in red and blue. It was magnificent. I also dug into my Latin repertoire and came up with the designation Purdey's 'Elixir Vitae' and the final presentation was perfect.

The only problem was that the newly decorated prototype bottle cost something like £2 a unit to produce on a small scale and Purdey's was due to retail at a hefty (for then) 99p. "Never mind", we thought. Once we got the volume up and worked on the bottle, IDV's technical geniuses would get the price down. And, of course, they did. And they did indeed ship the first case into Abbey Road studios, as planned, and Purdey's was up and running.

To top things off, I came up with the line 'More rhythm, less blues' which featured in all the promotional material for the Purdey's launch. On presenting it to Claire Watson for the first time, she looked at the work and said "Surely it should be fewer blues?" She was right, but then English was her first language. She good-naturedly let it go.

Purdey's generated a few urban myths as it was making its way. I remember a woman I knew telling me that she'd been up in Manchester

Side notes

There were a couple of interesting side notes on Purdey's. David (now Lord) Puttnam was said to be an enthusiast and that association triggered off the idea that we might make it available to film crews and rock bands. Lack of time and resources put paid to that. In a way we were going after the same territory as the now mega-brand Red Bull, although its owners didn't pussy-foot around with 'vitality' but offered a much harder option.

And there were also words between IDV's legal people and the gunsmiths, James Purdey & Son, about the use of their name. A photograph of Colin, beard and all, may have terminated that argument. And I'm surprised the producers of The Avengers TV series and their lawyers didn't try to hound us as well. (The female lead, played by Joanna Lumley, was called 'Purdy'.)

"

A trawl through *Culpeper's Complete Herbal* (Nicholas Culpeper was a 17th century English botanist, herbalist, physician and astrologer) unearthed the likes of bayberry bark extract, damiana, prickly ash bark and some B vitamins to produce the base for a recipe which IDV's technical group wove into another brilliant liquid."

Brand Purdey's 'Elixir Vitae'

USP Vitality without caffeine or sugar

Clients Claire Watson, Callitheke

Taste Vitamins, fruit with a hint of peach

Ideal drinkers Rock stars, actors

Launch 1988

Designer Howard Waller, Sedley Place

SPARKLING HERBAL MULTIVITAMIN
DRINK
PURDEY'S
elixir vitæ

INGREDIENTS: CARBONATED SPRING WATER, A BLEND OF PURE FRUIT JUICES, NATURAL FRUIT FLAVOURS, DAMIANA EXTRACT, BAYBERRY BARK EXTRACT, PRICKLY ASH BARK EXTRACT, CITRIC ACID, KOREAN GINSENG EXTRACT, VITAMIN C, CALCIUM PANTOTHENATE (B5), ZINC, VITAMIN B1, VITAMIN B6, SODIUM BENZOATE (PRESERVATIVE), VITAMIN B2, FOLIC ACID, VITAMIN B12

Waller's great shot at
making a complex message
comprehensible to normal people.

working and she had a couple of bottles on the train back to London and suddenly experienced substantial sexual arousal. Well, that's prickly ash bark for you. Others said that it was great with vodka – was this a forerunner of Red Bull? And, shades of Annie Greensprings 1960s US pop wine, Purdey's was regarded by some as the perfect accompaniment to marijuana. Maybe it was the damiana extract in the recipe that made the heart sing.

A few that got away
Callitheke was overheating

CALLITHEKE This was the umbrella company which we created for our range of drinks. The name was derived from classical Greek by Tim Ambler. The whole operation had become a real team effort and the name was a testament to Tim's hands-on commitment. Here was a main board director of a fast-growing global drinks company getting deeply involved in the fine detail of our little crusade. He was a true brand champion.

PFAFFS 'KALMWASSER' Purdey's was our version of an upper. Pfaffs was designed for people in the world of money – to help them wind down and chill out. By 1987 we were in the midst of Thatcher boom time and we felt that there might be an opportunity for a drink that would help high-powered market traders 'get away from it all'. It would be a kind of legal 'downer'. The basis for the formulation was a combination of camomile, passiflora and protein and, to highlight the product's calming character, we opted to present it as a thickened, opaque still product. In hindsight that was a mistake. The liquid was viscous, too heavy and filling, and definitely not something that people could drink in any quantity.

"

Purdey's was our version of an upper. Pfaffs was designed for people in the world of money – to help them wind down and chill out."

Brand Pfaffs 'Kalmwasser'

Name Jean-Marie Pfaff, Belgian goalkeeper

USP For the cool, calm and connected

Client Claire Watson, Callitheke

Taste Mixed fruit + protein – no fizz

Ideal drinker Gordon Gecko taking it easy

Launch Small-scale test 1990

Designer Howard Waller

There were two elements of which I was extremely proud. The name was really off-the-wall. We called it Pfaffs 'Kalmwasser' and designated it a 'protein fruit drink'. The name came while I was watching football on TV. England was playing Belgium and Jean-Marie Pfaff was the Belgian goalkeeper. It was a daring name and I loved the 'Pf which I

> We called it Pfaffs 'Kalmwasser' and designated it a 'protein fruit drink'. The name came while I was watching football on TV. England was playing Belgium and Jean-Marie Pfaff was the Belgian goalkeeper. It was a daring name and I loved the 'pf' which I thought might lead to some interesting 'underground' use like 'pf---ing pfantastic'."

thought might lead to some interesting 'underground' use like 'pf---ing pfantastic'. It was a pretty adventurous name and there were some detractors. It was, after all, the name of an internationally famous sewing machine company.

The other element that worked well was the strapline which I really liked. It was 'Pfaffs, for the cool, calm and connected'. But there was never time to get this one right and sadly it ended in 'pfailure'. None of us was at the top of our game for this one and even Waller's packaging was below his normal standard.

KHAVKA By 1990 we were beginning to move too quickly for our own good. Dexters was struggling through competition from heavyweight brand Lucozade Sport. Aqua Libra and Purdey's were moving along pretty well, but we were fragmenting management attention by looking at new brands like Pfaffs and a follow-up brand called Khavka. And alongside these developments, IDV had made an acquisition of an established health drink called Norfolk Punch. This put another brand into the Callitheke stable and also provided us with a dedicated production facility – with all its attendant expense.

We were doing a lot of reading, trawling through health magazines and looking at products in other fields like cosmetics and toiletries. We were steeping ourselves in the likes of Culpeper's. There was a lot of noise around about products for 'anti-ageing', especially in the skin-care sector, and the last brand developed for the Callitheke range was called Khavka which was based on betacarotene and anti-oxidant ingredients.

We were once again back to a carbonated product and IDV's research chemist Adrian Walker's liquid was based on the unusual blend of orange and beetroot. The taste was highly distinctive though perhaps not as challenging as Aqua Libra.

The name Khavka was derived from the Russian word 'Khavkas', meaning the Caucasus mountain range. Popular legend had it that pockets of people living in this region of Georgia enjoyed very long healthy lives. It would be a nice association. Mac Macpherson and I even took a trip to Tbilisi in 1990 to look for clues and secret ingredients. But, as so often happens when you make a deliberate attempt to look for ideas, all that emerged was some liver damage derived from the punishing Georgian hospitality. Our particular longevity was definitely not on our hosts' agenda.

IF ONLY... Innovation and product development has a high casualty rate and the fall of the house of Callitheke was one of the sadder moments in our business lives. It was sad because of the excitement we had enjoyed in setting it up. It was sad because of the great relationship we had with people at the top of the organisation. And it was especially sad because the ideas were so good.

I am an ideas man rather than a business analyst but I think we might have succeeded if only we had concentrated on the first three brands:

CALLITHEKE

GENEVA · PARIS · LONDON

Darrell Ireland's beautiful logo. And there's that Swiss thing again.

Dexters, Aqua Libra and Purdey's. They had achieved stellar beginnings and we should have focussed ruthlessly on building on that success. Instead, we got carried away with developing new ideas. In a way the travelling became more important than the arriving.

The 'company' grew too quickly. We had too many people and with the acquisition of Norfolk Punch we lumbered ourselves with overheads that were not sustainable. The Callitheke company with all its expensive baggage would have been better off if it had been absorbed into IDV's mainstream business as a single business unit, with manufacture being contracted out to a specialist soft drink bottler. To stand alone it needed to sell significantly more bottles.

The whole operation might have become viable if the company had acquired a mega-brand like Lucozade. This would have provided the volume and income to give Callitheke critical mass and enable it to secede from IDV's mainstream. Norfolk Punch was no big deal. And it came with a lot of baggage – a country house in Norfolk, acres of land, a production plant and the second largest bed in England known as 'the great bed of Diddington'.

But mergers and acquisitions were on the horizon, and even before IDV merged with Guinness United Distillers in 1997, Callitheke was dismantled in one of the earlier culls of businesses that were outside the corporate mainstream. It was sold for a song to a company that had been involved in bottling some of the products, Orchid Drinks in West Hartlepool. And from there it was later sold on to Britvic. I still see Purdey's in quite wide distribution in the UK these days – though my treasured 'Elixir Vitae' designation has bitten the dust. Dumbing it down, I suspect.

Dexters was hammered by the sheer weight of promotional spend which backed Lucozade Sport, and quietly disappeared. But the jewel in the crown, our magical brand Aqua Libra, seems to have vanished from sight. Maybe the current owners might consider bringing it back. It is a great brand and a reawakening might have surprising results.

Chapter Six
Whisky galore

Through much of my time whisky, and predominantly Scotch whisky, was the ultimate spirit. It was about heritage, maturity and sophistication. It was the drink to which you aspired and had to learn to appreciate. I loved working in whisky.

Whisky was my 'passport' category and took me to more countries than any other. I started in Scotland with The Singleton and then went on to Korea and Spain with J&B, Canada with Buffalo Jump and Jack Napier, India with Gilbey's Green Label and Ireland with Baileys 'The Whiskey'.

While the 'new-age' thinking that created Callitheke had its attractions – and challenges – I was to become increasingly enthusiastic about looking for new ideas in the more regulated sectors of the drinks business. The rules governing the production of pure vodka, for example, state that it must be 'colourless, odourless and flavourless'. (Flavoured vodkas represent a different category.)

And Scotch whisky posed even tougher challenges. The product has to age for at least three years and the whole process is governed by an act of the UK Parliament, the Scotch Whisky Act 1988.

J & B
Standing out from the crowd

Before the merger with Guinness United Distillers in 1997, J&B Rare was the Scotch jewel in the IDV crown. Starting life as a Scotch whisky which Justerini & Brooks gave to its wine customers at Christmas, it had been transformed by the American, Abe Rosenberg, to become the leading Scotch whisky in the US in the 1960s. But by Scotch whisky standards it was a very unusual brand.

I can remember seeing some consumer research which had been carried out on J&B in Italy in the 1970s. It didn't offer bags of encouragement to the company. These are some of the things Italian drinkers said about J&B and its bottle.

* The gaudy chartreuse and red label was completely out of keeping with the subdued elegance normally associated with the finest Scotch whiskies.
* The red top on the bottle made the whole package look cheap and ordinary and the green glass obscured the colour of the whisky, which people said looked 'watered down'.
* The Justerini name didn't help either. What do Italians know about making Scotch?
* And to cap it all, when these drinkers saw the product in a glass, their earlier 'watered down' perceptions were justified. It is much paler than more traditional whiskies such as Johnnie Walker, Bell's or Dewar's.

In today's research-obsessed business environment, the company might have made serious changes to the brand – or even dropped it for Italy. But fortunately for IDV, the J&B director, David Maxwell Scott, ignoring the research, went on with it as it was everywhere else in the world and it became a leading Scotch whisky in the Italian market. Intelligent judgment has it over research every time.

It also became a mega-brand in Spain where at one time it held over 40 per cent of the whisky market there. J&B in Spain was the largest brand-in-market in IDV.

A superb whisky. Pale and interesting.

Biker's Scotch

I can remember doing focus groups in Thailand and asking people what signals J&B emitted. One man said that it reminded him of 'biker's whisky'. It was macho and a bit 'show' and lacked the classic traditionalism of whiskies like Ballantine's and Johnnie Walker. It was an 'in-your-face Scotch' for people who were a bit different. I can just see Thai versions of Peter Fonda and Dennis Hopper 'easy riding' after a couple of J&Bs.

The J&B name also helped. It was easy to ask for and easy to remember. Interestingly, the Americans were never big on ampersands or apostrophes (a US colleague referred to Le Piat d'Or as 'Piat Dior') so J&B was usually pronounced simply 'JB' over there.

What J&B has is its distinctiveness. It is a bottle that really stands out in a crowd. But what people often forget in judging a whisky is its taste. Whisky is quite an intimate drink. People tend to be loyal to a brand and they become used to its taste. J&B Rare is a delicious whisky, a blend of 40-something of Scotland's finest malt and grain whiskies, skilfully put together to deliver a lovely soft, estery (floral/fruity) taste. It is the polar opposite to the harsher, smokier, phenolic whiskies like Johnnie Walker.

J&B's success in Spain was intriguing. Why should a Scotch whisky with an Italian name appeal to the Spanish? Was it the 'Jota B' name that made it an easy bar call? Or was there an association between J&B's red and yellow label and the Spanish flag? I suspect those things helped a little but its real success was probably due to the passion and skill of the Spanish sales team.

Super J&B
Jetting into Seoul

There was the beginning of a movement in the 1980s towards
'premiumising' drinks, and especially whiskies, and J&B was looking
for a 'super' version. It had a rather tired 12-year-old variant called J&B
Reserve but that didn't seem to be going anywhere. It was too stiff and
traditional and really out of keeping with the rebellious character that
seemed to personify J&B Rare. J&B's major competitor at the time was
Johnnie Walker and the IDV team wanted a J&B premium whisky that
stood a chance of tackling Johnnie Walker Black Label which, along
with Chivas Regal, dominated the premium sector.

It was a tough challenge and took some agonising over. But
eventually a dive into *Roget's Thesaurus* found the solution. The
problem was: 'How do we build a premium version out of J&B's unique,
almost iconoclastic reputation?' One of J&B's distinctive characteristics
is the prominent letter J. J occurs fairly infrequently in English words
which accounts for its high value in Scrabble. It is worth eight points
which places it just below the highest value letters Z and Q, both worth
ten points. Well, if you are desperate you have to start somewhere...

I found two words that looked interesting, 'Jade' and 'Jet' and
settled for the latter when I discovered that 'Jade' was being used by
the Cognac brand Otard. Then a picture began to form. Our main
target at that time was the Far Eastern markets of Thailand, Japan
and Korea. In those countries there is a tradition of 'hostess bars',
exclusive establishments where older businessmen could go to drink
and relax and be waited on by smart young ladies. These places are
very conservative in style and ruled over by owner-managers called
'Mama-sans'. Entertainment is pretty formal and the whisky costs an
arm and a leg.

They also have 'bottle-keeps' where they will mark your own personal bottle when you are finished with it for the evening, store it and bring it out when next you visit. A staid brand like J&B Reserve would fit into those conservative, dark-suited establishments. But this wasn't really what J&B Rare was about. We needed to do something different – a smart, premium version of an anti-establishment whisky.

J&B Jet was the proposal. It would be a premium Scotch whisky with a difference. It would aim to appeal to young, new-wave Far Eastern customers. It would be the 'Scotch to be seen with' among the smart set, people in IT, advertising and the entertainment business. Why would a cool 30-something dude from Seoul who wore a white suit, Ray-Bans at night, a Rolex Oyster and drove a Ferrari want to go out drinking to a place full of old guys being waited on by well-tailored, obedient women? Times were a-changing, even in downtown Tokyo, Bangkok and Seoul.

Designer Howard Waller was called in to do the design, as he had been on a number of projects. Although I did not attend the meeting, I gathered that his successful pitch for the business was based on showing two black snooker balls. He provided the essential logic behind the Jet name. Howard interpreted Jet as 'jet black' – a black bottle with a black label. It was stunning. And, given that IDV was locked in a fierce competitive battle with GuinnessUD, J&B Jet would be even 'blacker than black' – which in this context was arch-rival Johnnie Walker Black Label.

I loved J&B Jet because it was based on a single word from a thesaurus. Once we had the word, a brilliant designer like Howard Waller could transform it into something that really worked and set out to change the world.

This is one of the ideas that, at the time of writing, has not really made it yet except in one market, Korea. There it managed to open up what is now known as 'the modern on-trade', which comprised clubs and bars attracting trend-setting young drinkers. But it has not yet succeeded in making its mark in other countries. Sometime? Somewhere? Perhaps?

"

Howard interpreted Jet as 'jet black' – a black bottle with a black label. It was stunning. And, given that IDV was locked in a fierce competitive battle with GuinnessUD, J&B Jet would be even 'blacker than black' – which in this context was arch-rival Johnnie Walker Black Label."

Brand J&B Jet

Name Jet = jet black

USP The world's first modern Scotch

Client David Maxwell Scott, J&B

Taste J&B estery style with gravitas

Ideal drinker Young, hip IT and media types

Launch 1989

Designer Howard Waller

Imagine this block of (Perspex)
ice on a table in a smart bar
full of young, beautiful people.
Everyone would notice it.

Sticking to the Jet script
J&B goes sub-zero

The Koreans, having made a huge success of J&B Jet, now wanted a super-premium J&B to follow it. That's the way the whisky market goes in the Far East: the older and more expensive the whisky, the better drinkers believe them to be. What the Korean company really wanted was a 17-year-old or 21-year-old J&B to compete with other similarly aged brands like Ballantine's and Windsor.

My client at the time was Guy Escolme who managed J&B's business in Korea. He and I both felt that playing the age game was not J&B's style. It would be dragging it back into line with traditional, 'elderly' whiskies. Edgy, innovative J&B Jet had worked in Korea. In the search for a newer, even more premium J&B, I felt we should continue to startle and look for something perceptibly different from any other whisky. J&B, via Jet, was finding a new audience.

The seed for the idea that emerged had been planted some years before in a bar somewhere in the US. I was offered a gin martini served frozen, straight from the freezer. It was amazing. The gin was deliciously oily and viscous and the flavours of juniper, coriander and vermouth seemed to explode and envelop my tongue. It was a whole new glorious sensual experience. How might it work for a whisky? It would certainly be different.

I tried it at home by storing several glasses of whisky in my freezer and doing a taste test with a couple of friends. The results were interesting and quite unexpected. I had thought that the sweeter, estery J&B style would work really well when frozen. But it didn't happen that way. Smokier, phenolic Johnnie Walker blends seemed to deliver a much smoother, softer result. This was the reverse of my original expectation.

I always welcomed an idea which would present the company with a tough technical challenge. We had to go a lot further than simply suggesting that you could serve any Scotch straight from the freezer. I wanted our new super J&B to taste perceptibly better than any other Scotch whisky when it was served frozen. We needed a solution that was outstanding for the idea to work.

I named the whisky J&B Sub-Zero and brilliant designer Gordon Smith did a gorgeous bottle with a platinum label. Guy Escolme and I flew to Seoul to meet the company's Korean distributor, present the idea and test it in a few focus groups.

We were greeted by an assembly of about 25 executives, all dressed in dark navy blue suits. Out of respect we were similarly attired. I was introduced as the man who had created a host of liquor brands, including J&B Jet, which they had made a huge success in Korea, and for the first and last time in my career, my introduction was accompanied by a round of applause. They applauded again when I had finished presenting J&B Sub-Zero.

Gordon's bottle looked stunning and we also showed a special display piece in the form of a huge perspex block of ice which would contain the bottle and keep it frozen. Imagine what that would look like on a table in a smart bar or nightclub. Everyone would notice it. (The idea had been inspired by the early advertising for Gibbs SR toothpaste in the UK in the 1950s.)

There is a nice story in this vein attributed to Abe Rosenberg, the man who gave the title to this book. It was he who suggested that two flaming coffee beans should be served in a glass of Sambuca Romana when it was ordered in a bar or restaurant. "When do you blow out the flame?" a colleague asked. "When everyone in the restaurant has seen it" was the confident reply.

Guy and I retired to the bar after the presentation, leaving it to our Korean colleagues to discuss the idea with the management of the distribution company. We were feeling pretty confident. A round of applause was a rare thing after a sales pitch.

We waited about an hour before S G Ryu, our local representative, appeared. We were all agog. "How did they like it?" I asked excitedly. Ryu didn't know me too well and looked a little sheepish until he eventually blurted out "They hated it. They wanted a 17-year-old J&B. They said that people in Korea don't drink Scotch whisky straight from the freezer".

I said before that the problem with selling new ideas is not so much that people 'know what they like'. It's more a case of their 'liking what they know'. I still think that J&B Sub-Zero is an intriguing, innovative idea with huge potential. Famous Grouse had a Scotch for freezing on the market in the UK for a while but I'm not sure they put much drive behind it. I remain convinced that, if the technical challenge had been pursued, we could have emerged with the world's best frozen Scotch. Perhaps some enlightened manager will take it on.

Spey Royal
Purple for show

Most of the time in innovation, companies are looking for what they call 'added-value' premium products. They want to raise the ante with their brands by getting drinkers to trade up. But once in a while a brief comes along looking for more ordinary solutions. These challenges can be just as exciting as the more prestigious developments. And they are certainly a lot more demanding. It is a lot easier coming up with a solution when you throw money at it. Not so easy when there is very little in the bank.

There was major growth, especially in Europe, for value Scotch whiskies. White Horse, Clan Campbell and Vat 69 were making real inroads in markets like France, Italy and, particularly, Spain. And in this latter market another 'sub-prime' brand that was making good progress was a locally-produced Spanish whisky called DYC – pronounced 'Dick'. The name was an acronym for 'Destilerías y Crianza', a distillery established in Segovia in 1958. By the mid-1980s it had garnered a major following in Spain, one of Europe's largest whisky markets.

It must have been a decent product to pass muster in a country where brands like J&B, Johnnie Walker, Ballantine's and single malts like Cardhu did very good business. So, in view of the success of DYC and the presence of other lower-priced whiskies, Spain would become the test market for our new brand. It would be an interesting market because the Spanish liked drinking their whisky with cola.

Many of the elements in this venture were predetermined by the company, as their costs would be pared down to a minimum. We were told we could resurrect a dormant IDV Scotch brand called Spey Royal which had originally been created back in the early 1900s and had plodded along gathering dust in UK liquor stores in one form or another ever since. But it was a name. And it had heritage. These things were important for a Scotch whisky no matter how humble it might be.

The brief said that the whisky itself had to be young enough to be acceptable. Three years and a day would do – the minimum age required to allow you to call it Scotch whisky. We must stay with the existing Spey Royal bottle shape and the label dimensions had to be identical to those on the current bottle. A new label shape would require 'change-parts' for labelling machinery and those would be expensive. There was an element of Henry Ford's "You can have any colour you like – as long as it's black" about this brief.

What on earth could be done to produce a whisky that would give the Spanish whisky drinker an excuse to prefer it to White Horse, Vat 69 or DYC? The solution came from a trip around the spirits section of a very large supermarket in London. If you think about it, whiskies like White Horse, DYC or the new Spey Royal would fight their battle in large supermarkets, not in smart city bars, exclusive whisky shops or posh British stores such as Harrods or Fortnum & Mason. And in Spain the supermarkets are bigger than 'super', they're 'hyper'. These whiskies would occupy oceans of space on what they call 'gondola ends'. But the downside was that they would compete with thousands of items, from detergents to weed killers.

What a new, unfamiliar brand would need in one of these temples of retailing was to be conspicuous. In marketing terms, Spey Royal would need 'standout'. J&B Rare was probably the perfect model for this. Its

> The inspiration for new Spey Royal came from, of all unlikely places, the chocolate counter. The Cadbury's brand really stood out with its purple labelling. It was clearly differentiated from everything around it. And there was no purple on the whisky shelves."

Brand Spoy Royal 'Extra Rich'

USP Metallic purple label = strong standout

Client Jonathan Stordy, J&B

Taste Full-bodied standard Scotch

Ideal drinker Supermarket buyer – with attitude

Launch 1990

Markets Europe (intended), Thailand (actual)

Designers Darrell Ireland, Gerry Barney

red and yellow labelling really shouted from supermarket shelves. How could it be done again?

The inspiration for new Spey Royal came from, of all unlikely places, the chocolate counter. The Cadbury's brand really stood out with its purple wrapper. It was clearly differentiated from everything around it. And there was no purple on the whisky shelves.

That became the recommendation. Spey Royal must be noticed. Let's commission a stunningly beautiful purple label. In a field that is awash with pseudo-intellectual over-rationalisation, the idea that "We need standout, so let's go with a purple label" was pretty straightforward.

To my utter amazement, the company in the form of one Jonathan Stordy, now CEO of San Miguel in Madrid, bought the idea. The intellectual word for it in marketing jargon is 'insight'. It is an agreement of what the problem is. Once everyone is on the same wavelength, the rest is a lot easier.

And yet again going to school on other new brands, we asked the blenders for a full flavoured, dark whisky and signalled it on the label with the legend 'Extra Rich'.

Sadly, first time around Spey Royal died the death of a thousand focus groups. (Well, perhaps not that many.) The Spanish tried it in a half-hearted way but it didn't do much. The rest of Europe tested it among consumers who opined that "Whisky doesn't come in bottles with purple labels, so I wouldn't buy it". That was the point. Purple was different. Deliberately different. And the purple-haters were probably one motor-mouthed man and his obsequious side-kick.

The lesson? If you want someone to buy your product in a crowded supermarket, they have to see it first.

But the story, unexpectedly, ended on a good note. A very good note. Two entrepreneurs from Thailand, one a Thai and the other an expat Australian, somehow found out about Spey Royal. They flew to London and asked IDV if they could take on the brand in Thailand. There it would work perfectly, the dazzling purple colours projecting the livery of the Thai Royal family.

The rest is history. Spey Royal became the runaway brand leader in its sector and the two protagonists became millionaires. In a few years

IDV bought back the brand from them and the last I heard, they were relentlessly carrying out a 'de-purple-ising' programme.

I loved Spey Royal because it created something out of very little. And while it did not bring immediate short-term success to IDV, it made a couple of very pleasant entrepreneurs very rich and very happy. Thailand was, I suppose, a special case though I remain convinced that Spey Royal would have worked everywhere else.

Taking the pain out of single malt
A malt for blend drinkers

The longer I worked in the drinks business the more interesting certain categories became. It was a good 15 years before there was a chance to work in malt whisky. In the 1980s IDV had only one single malt, Knockando, and the company was quite precious about it. These whiskies were the spirit equivalents of fine chateau wines such as Lafite and Latour. They were aloof, subdued in their presentation and in taste terms not very accessible to uninitiated drinkers. It was more often a case of the producer deigning to allow the humble consumer access to their magnificent products. The French were especially good at that kind of thing.

By the mid-1980s a few malts were beginning to break out of the pack and sell to a larger audience. Most notable contenders were Glenfiddich (from William Grant), The Glenlivet and an emerging Macallan. And perhaps the most interesting of all was another malt from the Grant's stable called Glen Grant.

Unlike most malts which I described above as 'chateau Scotch', Glen Grant was a mid-priced single malt that had taken the Italian market by storm. Here was a single malt competing with mainstream brands and its advertising line 'Puro Malto' was the foundation upon which its success was built. It seemed to strike a very positive chord with Italian whisky drinkers. And Glen Grant wasn't only taking business from other malt whiskies: it was also appealing to blended whisky drinkers. It was a malt with an accessible taste. That was our conclusion when we tasted it, I think at about 10.30 one cold London February morning.

IDV wanted a piece of this action. The hunt was on for a new immediately palatable single malt, and one that would be aimed at blended Scotch drinkers. This was an interesting challenge because malts were invariably based on location. Where they came from was an integral component of what they were. And IDV was not about to buy a new distillery.

The idea that eventually emerged was based on a series of fairly straightforward observations. Firstly, we must be true to our aim to create a malt to appeal to blended Scotch drinkers. We needed a product that was smooth and sweet and not too punishing to drink. It shouldn't require too much learning, like big hitters Laphroaig and Lagavulin. These are complex, challenging malts that need a lot of 'sip time' before you learned to appreciate them.

We were lucky enough to have just such a malt on the doorstep at IDV's own distillery on Speyside called Auchroisk (pronounced 'Orth rusk'). It was a signature component in J&B Rare and it had that lovely, estery, floral flavour that was the key to J&B's success. It was exactly the kind of taste profile we were after.

Looking at the available malts on the market, most of the whiskies themselves were very pale in colour. And paleness could signal either astringency or weak, watered-down flavour. To make our new malt more inviting, we should aim for a rich, satisfying, full-bodied appearance. We would achieve this through the addition of caramel, the standard method of darkening (and standardising) whisky colour and to enhance its richness of taste we would finish the malt in sherry casks, another traditional method of maturing a whisky.

An inspection of malt packaging was very similar to the review of French wines that we did for Le Piat d'Or back in the early seventies (see Chapter 3). Design was very laid back and understated – several plain white labels with black type. It didn't signal to average drinkers that malt was a bit special and justified its premium price over their

Bringing some glitz to the malt whisky sector.

Distillery visits were an obligation in the drinks business. And despite my technical ineptitude, I learned enough to reap some useful dividends.

normal Scotch. This unassuming presentation also made malts pretty well invisible to the ordinary drinker. Glenfiddich had broken that mould and was doing very well, but the rest were shyly lurking in the dark recesses of most liquor stores. We would look to offer a tasteful but more obviously premium presentation.

This looked like becoming Le Piat d'Or or even Croft Original all over again. It would be an easy, enjoyable product but beautifully made, with obviously premium labelling. It would stand out like a beacon of quality in among the fuddy-duddy old fashioned establishment malts. It would be a malt for the new whisky drinker, in America, in Thailand and in Japan. And we would call it The Singleton.

About six months into launch we enjoyed an amazing stroke of good

The Singleton – *the* single malt

Our last problem creating this single malt was with the name. We had only one distillery name we could use and that was likely to be impossible for anyone to pronounce. That name was Auchroisk. Remember, we were trying to create 'the people's malt', a whisky that spoke the language of ordinary blended Scotch whisky drinkers.

In the search I dug up a name that we had used a couple of times in the past. It was Singleton or The Singleton as it later became. That touch of pomposity seemed to fit malt whisky. First, there was Singleton's Gin for a project we did in the early seventies. And a few years later we experimented with Baileys Singleton, a one-shot ready-to-drink product based on Baileys, vanilla and milk.

Neither idea got off the drawing board. But Singleton worked for a malt, everyone in the team loved it and The Singleton of Auchroisk was launched in the UK in 1985. And a subsequent serendipitous discovery was that the term 'singleton' was actually part of the language of malt whisky buying in the early years of the 20th century so this gave further justification to the name. You could buy malt whisky by the single cask, or 'singleton'.

fortune. The *Sunday Express* was running a 'Best of British' competition covering three drink categories – beer, cider and malt whisky. Someone entered our product in to a tasting competition judged by a group of the UK's best known Scotch whisky aficionados. All the most famous brands were featured and, in some instances, their 'top-shelf' versions were submitted.

To our delight The Singleton won the competition and the drinks writer Oz Clarke wrote a brilliant piece extolling the virtues of the product. This was important to us. It is all very well getting the thinking right but product excellence was everything. The stuff in the bottle had to be the best it could be. A positive vote from such an august audience was just what we needed.

But perhaps winning this award had a negative effect on the early development of The Singleton. It went to our heads and the brand was priced significantly above the level which we had originally intended. Instead of sitting between premium blends like Chivas Regal and Johnnie Walker Black and the top shelf malts, it was priced too high. It plodded along during the 1990s without attracting too much attention. In fact there were times when I was surprised it managed to stay alive at all.

In 2006, after I had stopped working for Diageo, I was hired as a consultant to look at malt whisky in Taiwan where the category was beginning to grow. I managed to persuade the local team to feed The Singleton into the mix of whiskies that were being studied and as a result of research carried out in that market, the brand was re-launched with a beautiful new package designed by master craftsman Gerry Barney from Sedley Place. It was he who had designed the original Singleton.

It appeared initially as The Singleton of Glen Ord, then as Glendullan, and is now marketed as The Singleton of Dufftown. Most recent intelligence suggests that it is one of the star brands in the company's malt whisky portfolio and its ability to carry a variety of distillery names adds to its distinctiveness and commercial appeal. The name can be applied to any distillery which has a surplus of malt whisky stocks.

Baileys 'The Whiskey'?
Sadly not

Perhaps the most intriguing whisky development came in 2001 after a summons to Dublin from the new CEO of Baileys, Chris Britton, who had cut his teeth on building Malibu. In its earliest days, Malibu was simply a coconut-flavoured white spirit. It had no heritage or authenticity. Chris's great achievement involved relocating Malibu to Barbados and using Bajan rum as part of the product's spirit base.

This provided the solid foundations Malibu needed to enable it to achieve major global brand status. It became so successful that Diageo sold it to Allied Domecq for £560 million in 2002 when they merged with Seagram's and acquired the Captain Morgan Rum brand. The Monopolies & Mergers Commission, interestingly, classified Malibu as a rum and Diageo carried too many rums for the health of the category.

On taking over Baileys, Chris arrived at a similar conclusion to that which he had identified for Malibu. Baileys was simply an assembly of flavours in an undefined spirit base. If Baileys could be invested with premium spirit credentials, it would help him to take the brand to the next level. What he called "spirit values" meant a better, more prestigious product and ultimately a higher price for the company.

To achieve this we would do a Baileys whiskey. An Irish whiskey. That was the originally conceived spirit base for the very first Baileys and Chris saw no reason to depart from that.

The people assigned to this task were to feature prominently in the latter stages of my business career. David Phelan, very experienced, ran it from the Baileys end and Adrian Walker, one of the best product people I ever worked with, was the Diageo innovation team representative. It was he who had the breakthrough idea.

As Scotch whisky fans will know, a variety of methods are available to finish a product. Most blends are matured in used oak bourbon barrels.

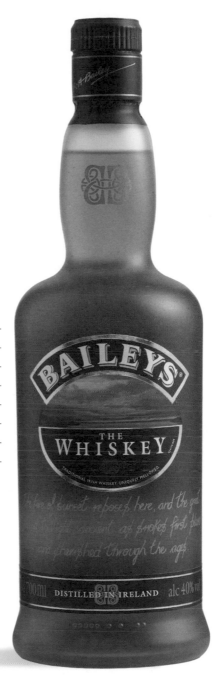

"

The whiskey could go into the Baileys product as part of its spirit base. But the breakthrough idea was that we should store the Baileys' flavours in oak bourbon casks and then tip these out and fill the casks with whiskey."

Brand Baileys 'The Whiskey'	
USP Matured in Baileys flavour barrels	
Clients Chris Britton, Baileys	
Taste Mellow Irish, hint of chocolate	
Ideal drinker Whiskey novices	
Launch Not really	
Designer Terry Green at Design Factory	

Baileys Whiskey Comes to Town

Irish company R&A Bailey has recently introduced Baileys Whiskey onto the market. *John Corrigan* interviewed their brand manager, Noel Whelan, on this bold new move.

Irish company R&A Bailey has recently introduced Baileys Whiskey onto the market. We interviewed their brand manager, Noel Whelan, on this bold new move.

"Whiskey has always been at the heart of Baileys Irish Cream," said Whelan. "It gives our product its unique taste and character. And only the very best Irish whiskey goes into Baileys. In fact over the years it has been a tradition of ours to give special bottles of the whiskey we use to our most favoured customers around the world. In fact it has been so well received that we have now decided to make it more widely available.

Whelan then went on to describe the taste of the product : "Some have described it as 'the Baileys of Irish whiskey'. It's full and mellow and very more-ish, with a wonderful, almost comforting smoothness on the palate. We are proud to allow it to carry the Baileys name.

Our Off-Licence News taste panel put it to the test as Mr Whelan was kind enough to give us a bottle. The consensus was highly favourable and we could see the logic behind the idea. The Baileys name and reputation do bring a lot to an Irish whiskey.

But we wondered how it would be viewed by committed Baileys Irish Cream users. How would they feel about a whiskey product being sold in the pubs and off-licences alongside their Irish Cream. Will it cause confusion?

Baileys Whiskey is available in selected outlets and it will be interesting to see how it will be received when it achieves wider distribution. It is priced at £13.99 a bottle.

The very first communication of the Baileys Whiskey idea – before we came up with the name, pack design or the idea of maturing in Baileys flavour casks.

These become available because bourbon has to be matured in new oak, so each barrel can only be used once. Some whiskies are aged in sherry casks (Macallan and The Singleton) while port pipes and Madeira casks have also been used. And there have been occasions, though many years ago, where some whiskies were even finished in beer barrels.

Adrian's solution was even more radical. This was to be a Baileys whiskey, so there should be some genuine connection with the parent brand. Well, the whiskey could go into the Baileys product as part of its spirit base. But his breakthrough idea was that we should store the Baileys' flavours in oak bourbon casks and then tip these out and fill the casks with whiskey. If it was OK to age whisky in port pipes or sherry casks where some of the original product flavour would be imparted, why not these Baileys-flavoured casks? I thought it was an amazing idea – beautifully simple and potentially legal.

We made some product and tested the idea among Irish drinkers. They really liked it and it was seen as either 'Baileys for men' or 'whiskey for women'. The liquid did particularly well and people could pick out the gentle hint of Baileys in the taste and bouquet. There was a lovely synergy between the two products which really worked in the glass.

This magazine article on the opposite page is the way Baileys 'The Whiskey' was first introduced to Irish drinkers. It was accompanied by a product created by Adrian Walker. The package design followed once we knew where we were going.

A contribution of mine of which I was particularly proud was the name. I can remember writing it on the paper tablecloth at a Chinese restaurant the night before a key presentation. We called it Baileys 'The Whiskey' which seemed very Irish. Phelan and Walker both loved it and when anyone questioned it, the argument went something like this: a man goes into a bar and asks for a Baileys (unspecified). The barman says "cream or whiskey?" The man says "whiskey". And that's how it might play out. If creating an extension to an existing brand, try to keep the original name in play. If the 'sub-name' is too powerful – Sapphire in Bombay Sapphire perhaps – the original name can get swamped.

I particularly enjoyed the process of selecting a designer for this brand. David Phelan was the client at the time and was keen to employ an Irish design company for a change, so we invited a Dublin group called Design Factory to tender for the business. We knew these designers had no premium spirits in their product portfolio so this would be a whole new ball game for them.

They won the pitch by using a range of toilet brushes to illustrate their argument. I can't remember the exact train of thought, but it was pretty courageous. After a few early skirmishes we became quite concerned about their ability to produce a great design but were delighted with the final result.

This is another idea that didn't make it. It launched in Ireland and initial responses were highly favourable. But its legality was questioned by both the Irish and Scotch Whisky Associations. At the time Diageo was in the process of merger talks with Seagram's. Pragmatic thinking prevailed and Baileys 'The Whiskey' was quietly withdrawn. It was too prominent a diversion when more important things were in play.

Canadian mellow-mash whisky
Buffalo Jump has its head smashed in

As IDV grew larger and more successful, so it looked to either acquire or develop brands in categories where it wasn't represented. In the early 1990s bourbon whiskey was it – huge in the US and growing in Europe. The category was dominated by brands like Jim Beam and Jack Daniel's, though the latter is not strictly classified as bourbon as it isn't produced in Kentucky. It is designated a 'Tennessee sipping whiskey'.

The company didn't have a Bourbon on its books, though it owned large reserves of Canadian whisky. Outside of North America, perhaps to the English and other Europeans, bourbon and Canadian whiskies could easily be made to merge into the broad description of 'North American whiskey'. Bourbon generally came in squat, square bottles, had a distinctive smoky-sweet flavour and had a relaxed rural image. It also went very well with Coca Cola. What would happen if we developed a Canadian whisky with those characteristics?

I started with the product description and came up with the term 'mellow mash'. This was a variation on 'sour mash' which described many well-known American whiskies. Mellow mash seemed a nice variation on that theme and would set up the expectation of a smoother, more palatable whisky. And that is what we would deliver.

Moreover, it would be possible because the laws governing the production of Canadian whisky allowed the addition of up to 9 per cent of flavoured materials like prune juice, or even port or sherry. That is because the Canadians produced rye or grain whisky which was lighter in flavour and character than malted whiskies. The introduction of additives would provide the opportunity to manipulate the taste of the whisky and give it a more 'substantial' flavour. IDV's development team produced a liquid that tasted every bit as good as Jim Beam or Jack Daniel's – some thought even better. It certainly delivered the mellow-mash promise, which we emblazoned on the label.

Name and package were the last pieces in the puzzle and I found the former during a deep dive into a map of Canada. Just north of Fort MacLeod in Alberta, there is a World Heritage site called Head-Smashed-In Buffalo Jump. It is an archaeological site known around the world as a testimony to the life of the Plains peoples. The 'Jump' bears witness to a method of hunting practised by native people of the North American plains for nearly 6,000 years. Head-Smashed-In Buffalo Jump did what it said on the tin. Drive the buffalo to the cliff, force them to jump and you've got food and clothing for a couple of years.

Buffalo Jump: we loved it. The 'Head-Smashed-In' part probably wouldn't go down too well with the anti-alcohol lobbies. But the last part worked. And to communicate Canada's wide open spaces, I developed the line 'Free Range Prairie Whisky'.

Sadly our buffalo was another one that got away. I can remember trying to sell it in South Africa and Japan. But it wasn't bourbon and didn't carry all the history and tradition of Scotch, so we couldn't make a sale. Some thought that the 'buffalo' connection made it sound too 'menacing', though Buffalo Trace, a bourbon from Kentucky, seems to do quite well these days.

Gilbey's Green Label Rich Blend Whisky
A victory to logic and logistics

India was an area of interest to IDV for a number of years and Mac Macpherson, my partner in crime at IDV after Tom Jago departed, and I went on an exploratory mission to Bombay (as it was then) and Delhi in 1984. Legend had it that the company had a look every decade, thought about it and then opted out. And our first visit was no exception. It was a pity because we really enjoyed the trip and loved the people. And we learned a lot too.

The world's first 'mellow-mash' whiskey would be like Bourbon but different.

FINEST QUALITY

PRODUCT OF CANADA

ORIGINAL OLD STYLE

MELLOWED IN THE BARREL

BUFFALO JUMP

CHARCOAL FILTERED

MELLOW-MASH

Canadian Rye Whiskey

AGED IN WHITE OAK BARRELS

AGED 8 YEARS

43% ALC/VOL   ウイスキー

750 ML

DISTILLED BY PRAIRIE DISTILLERS

Then in the early 1990s the company got serious. It appointed a senior local drinks man, Deepak Roy, to set up a business initially from offices in the palatial Oberoi hotel in Mumbai. The category we would develop was whisky because Indian whisky was by far the largest spirit category. It was a hugely competitive market dominated by some very big players and it would be a real challenge for us to compete. Having someone with Deepak's experience and local knowledge was crucial in getting this thrilling venture off the ground.

We spent a lot of time looking at market data and even more time out in the field, visiting bars and liquor stores. We tasted a lot of products which were OK but more like rum than Scotch – which is not surprising given their molasses base. But we built up an awareness of the kind of flavour profiles that Indian drinkers liked. Alan Wilton was a top product developer in IDV's innovation team and we set our sights on producing better-crafted, better-tasting whiskies than anything available in India at the time. This was the sine qua non of our venture.

It was an inspection of bottles and labels, however, that really gave rise to the big idea. These whiskies were bought by Indians on relatively low incomes. And low incomes in Indian terms were a lot lower than US or European low incomes. By any standards these people were poor. We should look to create real mass market brands.

The existing packages we saw in our travels around the country looked very shoddy indeed. The bottles were badly presented, labels were dog-eared and badly printed and often stuck on upside down. The glass bottles themselves were full of flaws. And products were variable from bottle to bottle and on occasion aroused genuine health scares.

Our idea was to use all the technological expertise and muscle that IDV had at its disposal to produce a range of Indian whiskies which looked every bit as good as the best international brands. Put simply, why should inexpensive whiskies look cheap? This became an exercise in project management rather than innovatory thinking and there was no one better than Alan Wilton to handle this.

Our start point was design and we commissioned 'Design-Waller' to operate as if he was creating a super-premium brand. Then we arranged that all the printing plates and colour separations would be produced in London so that we were able to exercise the closest possible control over the quality of label printing. And we applied the same focused approach to the creation of bottle moulds. We wanted our bottle to look comfortable on a shelf at Harrods or behind the bar at the Rose Club in New York's Plaza hotel.

Once the groundwork had been completed, Wilton and his team flew to India and located bottle makers and printers who could produce to the standards we were after. Waller too could be merciless when it came to implementing his design work. And then IDV installed stringent quality control systems in the distillery to ensure that the very highest standards were met at all levels of production of the product itself.

The whisky was marketed under the Gilbey's brand. CEO Deepak Roy wanted an international stamp for his whiskies but the SWA would

Retailing Delhi-style

The stores In India were a real culture shock. Their interpretation of Zimmerman's of Chicago or London's Whisky Exchange was a tumbledown shack with case after case of booze piled one on top of the other. And lying atop these mountains of cases were one or two painfully thin gentlemen whose remit was to clamber, rummage and then extract selected cases from the pile and deliver them up to an expectant customer.

The products were interesting too. Most of the boxes contained whisky. Indian whisky. But you wouldn't think so if you read the names. Bagpiper, Peter Scot, Royal Challenge and McDowell's No 1 did not make for a particularly subcontinental array. Most were Scotch 'look-alikes' and while some were 'admixes', which meant they contained a small quantity of Scotch in the overall blend, others were plain Indian whiskies.

And Indian whisky is made from molasses, not grain. Over the years the Indians have driven the Scotch Whisky Association (SWA) apoplectic with their fluid interpretation of the word 'whisky'. But it hasn't helped. India powers on as one of the largest 'whisky' markets in the world.

We wanted our bottles to look
comfortable on a shelf at Harrods
or behind the bar at the Rose
Club in New York's Plaza Hotel."

Brand Gilbey's Green Label 'Rich Blend' Whisky

USP Local whisky, world class presentation

Client Deepak Roy, International Distillers, India

Taste Exceptionally smooth, consistent flavour

Ideal drinker Men who aspired to imported whisky

Launch 1999

Designer Howard Waller

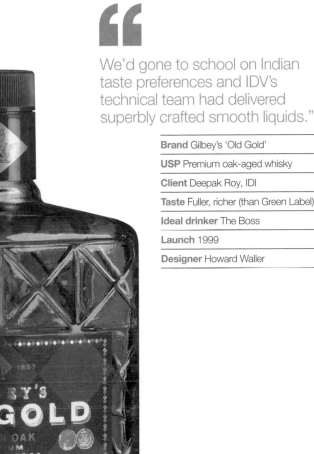

" We'd gone to school on Indian taste preferences and IDV's technical team had delivered superbly crafted smooth liquids."

Brand Gilbey's 'Old Gold'

USP Premium oak-aged whisky

Client Deepak Roy, IDI

Taste Fuller, richer (than Green Label)

Ideal drinker The Boss

Launch 1999

Designer Howard Waller

The Indian retail scene was gloriously chaotic: case piled upon case with willing 'rummagers' delving amongst the stock to find your brand of choice. I loved it.

Cultural differences

I travelled the world creating new styles of whisky. Of all the people I studied, Korean men were best able to identify quality Scotch. They would drink it in large measures, on ice or with a little water, so they liked the taste. I remember blind-testing a 12-year-old quality Scotch against a 'no age' cheap brand and all my Korean respondents preferred the 12. They knew it was better quality. The Spanish drink it with Coke, while the Scots, horror of horrors, drink it with lemonade. Many Far Eastern drinkers are obsessed with aged Scotch, the older the better, though I have been told by experts in the field that 12 years is about the optimum age. Older than that and the whisky gets 'tired' and develops too much wood flavour.

not permit the use of an established Scotch brand name on a locally produced 'Scotched-up' molasses product. Although known now for gin and vodka, the Gilbey's name had been around since 1857 and the company was one of the great pioneers in the international export of alcoholic beverages.

The result of our efforts was a range of Gilbey's whiskies, the star performer being Gilbey's 'Green Label' which would operate in the mass market slot. We also developed a premium variant called Gilbey's 'Old Gold'. And we'd gone to school on Indian taste preferences and IDV's technical team had delivered superbly crafted smooth liquids.

We were overjoyed with the result: the packs looked stunning based on a Gilbey's 'diamond' motif that Howard had unearthed and appropriated. They would have graced the smartest bars in London, New York or Mumbai. The company was launched in 1994 and was a major success, reaching three million 12-bottle cases within two years. Deepak's management had been a triumph.

By 2002 IDV had become Diageo and had switched focus from local brands to global giants like Johnnie Walker. The Indian company was sold to V J Mallya's United Breweries and Green Label was re-presented under the McDowell's brand. (I don't think the new packaging holds a candle to Waller's original.) It currently sells around three million cases, which puts it among the top 12 Indian whiskies. That's pretty big business. Most recent information indicates that Diageo have taken a major share in India United Spirits, owners of Green Label, so perhaps it will enjoy a new lease of life.

The wonderful subcontinent
India was one of my dream jobs

India was a marvellous experience. We visited and did focus groups in Mumbai, Delhi, Calcutta, Ludhiana, Bangalore, Cochin and Trivandrum and learned how Indian drinkers enjoyed their 'pegs'. We socialised with the people and revelled in the colours and sounds of the subcontinent. I could hardly believe that I was being paid to do all this. And I was able to do most of the focus groups myself. India has over 400 languages and English always turned out to be the default language when a group of whisky drinkers got together.

Focus groups in India did have their moments. I can recall one occasion in Mumbai when twelve people from the company and their advertising agency observed a group through CCTV while sitting on a double bed in the next room. And another, when we observed a group in Hindi through a hatch between a tiny kitchen and a dining room. The kitchen, the size of a telephone kiosk, had the same dozen people, plus me and a simultaneous translator.

Chapter Seven
Chasing the
great white

1969–2005 Green Island Mauritius Rum * Kenya Cane *
Stubbs Australian White rum * Smirnoff Black Super-Smooth vodka
* Tanqueray Ten fresh botanical gin * Ciroc Grape vodka

White spirits like vodka, gin and rum were to occupy a great deal of my career in the drinks business. And with mixed success. We never managed to challenge Bacardi successfully, but vodka and gin were another story.

The problem of coming up with something totally new in vodka, a category where the product had to be colourless, odourless and flavourless, really did concentrate the mind.

I greatly enjoyed building a story for Smirnoff Black, based on the legend '1818' staring at me from the shoulder of the bottle. The date led to a pot-still product which in turn yielded the world's smoothest vodka.

Gin, being essentially a flavoured spirit, offered greater opportunity.

It had all started back in 1969 during my first encounter with Tom Jago, who was my port of entry into IDV and the wonderful world of drink. At the time Tom was a kind of 'innovator without portfolio' for the company.

IDV wanted a rum, a white rum, to compete with Bacardi, which was then marching inexorably towards becoming the largest-selling spirit brand in the world. It was my first encounter with the drinks business and after working for a month Tom suggested that we take a trip to Mauritius and South Africa with a brief stop-off in Kenya (Nairobi) en route. I was beginning to endure the hardships of working in the industry.

The journey bore fruit in the development of three brands and, while they are still around nearly 50 years on, none of them has shown any great inclination to venture outside their original habitats.

Green Island rum
The first drink we ever created

The first product of our labours was a Mauritian white rum called Green Island which was launched on the island in 1972. It was the first drink of any kind that we ever created. One small discovery of which I was extremely proud was the location of a quote about Mauritius penned by Mark Twain in his book *Following the Equator* which read: "You gather the idea that Mauritius was created first, and then heaven; and that heaven was copied after Mauritius".

These words appeared on the Green Island label and, as far as I know, have remained there ever since. There was a bit of licence in using the quote, as Twain referred to it in the context of Mauritians' tendency to

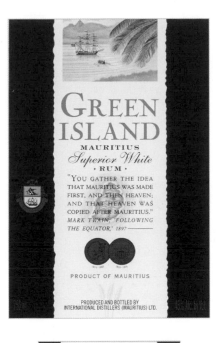

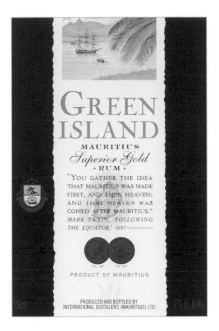

Darrell Ireland's exceptional Green Island graphics.

The Mauritius telegram

There was an amusing side story to the Green Island development. The distillery was opened near Port Louis, the capital of Mauritius, in 1972 and during the ceremony Robin Kernick, the chairman of IDV, was approached by the Governor-General of Mauritius and asked about the '1849' date that had originally appeared on the neck label of the bottle.

Mr Kernick had no idea of its significance and soon the wires between Port Louis and IDV's in London head office were trilling. Tom Jago was away somewhere and I seemed to be the only person who knew the answer. I was eventually located and explained that it was the date of issue of the famous Mauritius Penny Black stamp and it had been included to add a little history to the brand. Well, it was our first ever brand and there wasn't a hell of a lot we could find to say about Mauritius. Dodos were unlikely to motivate rum drinkers.

overhype their country. But it seemed like a good idea at the time – and when we visited there, Mauritius was indeed an idyllic green island.

The inclusion of quotes like that was intended to give a brand personality and heritage. Green Island was a new rum but it needed to exude some of the reassurance of seeming to have been around a long time. Although I have come across Green Island in the odd specialist liquor store in London, the rum never really left Mauritius. We had high hopes of at least biting at Bacardi's substantial ankles but it never really happened.

Sunny tropical beaches surrounded by palms provided the signature for white rum. Close your eyes and think of Bacardi.

Something for Africa
Not a chance

Two other drinks emerged from this trip via a brief stopover in Nairobi en route. We met the head of IDV's Kenya company and he asked whether we could create a local drink for export. Kenya was probably the only African country at that time (1969) which might provide a credible source for an alcoholic drink. It was well known as a safari destination, it had fine game parks and had been featured in books like Hemingway's *Snows of Kilimanjaro*.

Following the stopover in Nairobi the first African drink we created was a cane spirit – a kind of un-aged rum – based on a category which was hugely successful in South Africa. We called it Kenya Cane which had a nice alliterative ring to it. The bottle was designed by Kit Cooper from London design consultancy Sedley Place.

The second Kenyan drink was a natural – a coffee liqueur based on that country's wonderful 'high mountain' Arabica coffee bean. It was a gorgeous liqueur in a bottle designed by Gerry Barney, also from Sedleys.

It is over 40 years since these drinks were created and neither appears to have attracted any interest outside Kenya. Come to think of it, interest inside Kenya has been pretty low-key.

We tried very hard to help get Kenya Cane off the ground and I can remember making an arrangement with a German importer to ship 1,200 bottles to Munich. It took the Kenyans about two years to supply product by which time I suspect the clients had lost interest.

"

The first African drink we created was a cane spirit – a kind of un-aged rum – based on a category which was hugely successful in South Africa. We called it Kenya Cane which had a nice alliterative ring to it."

Brand Kenya Cane

USP A taste of the (African) wildlife

Client Ralph Bond, Gilbeys Kenya

Taste Un-aged rum

Ideal drinker Papa Hemingway

Launch 1972, but never really left Kenya

Designer Kit Cooper, Sedley Place

The $64,000 question
Another shot at beating Bacardi

We had tried once before with Green Island and here we were again 15 years later in 1985 having another go. "How can we come up with an idea for a white rum that can really attack Bacardi?" was the challenge IDV gave me. I loved tasks like that. Bacardi was huge and seemingly perfect. How do we find a chink in its armour?

IDV handled Smirnoff vodka distribution outside the US for many years until it bought its parent company, Heublein, in 1987 which gave it access to that market too. Throughout my time working with IDV there was a fascination with Bacardi rum since Bacardi and Smirnoff were slugging it out to become the world's biggest-selling spirit brand.

The first task was to read a lot: articles, advertisements, research reports. How do we discover the essence of Bacardi? Then I did a couple of focus groups, just one evening, one with men and the other with women. I listened to Bacardi fans talk about the brand. I even tossed in a 'blind' tasting where people compared Bacardi and Coke

Remembrance of things past

Bacardi was an almost mythical brand to me growing up. I read about it in Hemingway novels, *For Whom the Bell Tolls* and *The Old Man and the Sea*, and saw it advertised in American magazines. It represented an unattainable romance to a young man in faraway South Africa. I never saw it there in my early drinking days. Yet here I was, trying to attack it with a new brand.

with Smirnoff and Coke. They didn't know what they were drinking but could they tell the difference? This exploration took about a month in all. Then it was time to get off the pot.

Like many ideas, it happened when I was lying in bed, just awake at about 6am. All the pieces in the puzzle seemed to come together with a comforting click. Wow!

What had been learned about Bacardi? The first observation was that it appealed equally to men and women. It was the universal spirit.

Bacardi was also about the islands, tropical paradises with palm trees, clean, golden beaches populated by slim, bronzed beautiful people. Barbados, Jamaica, Seychelles, Cuba? Mauritius even? Who knew? They all looked much like one another. Also, looking at Bacardi bottles, it was clear that the rum was bottled all over the place. It might be produced in Spain, or the Philippines, or Puerto Rico or even Indonesia. Although the whole Bacardi environment was about tropical islands, it might be bottled in an industrial suburb outside Madrid or Manila.

There were a few interesting discoveries about the product as well. It was perceptibly sweeter than vodka. With Coke it was thought to be very sweet indeed. And at 38% alcohol it was below the standard level for stronger spirits like whisky, brandy and gin.

So, our formula was in place. Bacardi had strong feminine appeal, so we would devise a new rum that would bypass this and target its masculine side. How do you produce a more masculine rum? Well, we would start with the product, the stuff in the bottle: it would be significantly drier in taste, not as molasses-sweet as Bacardi. Then, we would make it stronger, higher in alcohol – and we arbitrarily stipulated 43%, a hefty 5% above Bacardi. Those elements would add up to a more masculine product.

The last piece in the puzzle was 'where?' Where would we make it? Was there a place somewhere that produced sugar cane but didn't look like it was another 'Bacardi-land'? That meant no Caribbean islands or look-alikes such as Mauritius, the Maldives or the Seychelles. And though Africa was on the tropic line previous experience suggested that it was a no-no. Sugar was tropical so I traced lines through Capricorn and Cancer and found the perfect place – Australia. Australia was about as macho as you could get and it had recently been put on the map by the film *Crocodile Dundee* which was taking America by storm. Paul Hogan was as far from the archetypal Bacardi drinker as it was possible to be. We also found a product edge. We could make our rum from freshly pressed cane juice, not treacly molasses, like most other rums e.g. Bacardi.

Mac Macpherson was running brand development at IDV at that time and he and his team put out some feelers and we found a willing partner, a small independent distillery at Beenleigh which was situated outside Brisbane en route to the Queensland Gold Coast. Being enthusiastic 'can do' Aussies they were happy to join in and said that they would have no problems with sourcing fresh cane juice and producing a lovely dry, strong Australian white rum. We called it Stubbs, another name from our archive. The design was stunning: another Howard Waller original though rather more traditional than his usual efforts.

We took great care of the details in this design and I included a legend on the cap which read 'First for Thirst' which was the kind of language that might have appeared on drinks packages at the turn of the 20th century. It was corny, but good corny. Then, as a subtle dig at Bacardi, we put the line 'Made only in Australia' in red type above the brand name on the label.

What I have learned is that if you look really closely at all aspects of a brand when you design it, you can turn some of the most mundane things into selling elements. No tiny detail was too small to be ignored in this venture.

So far, so good. The most enjoyable parts of the Stubbs campaign had been solving the problem and creating the brand. But everything went downhill after that. We could not engage the local Australian company in selling it in their market, which would be the Stubbs homeland. We had foolishly not involved them in any part of the development process so corporate noses were put out of joint.

That kind of thing happens. For example, while Foster's lager was a prominent Australian beer in the UK, it was rarely visible in its home

"

How do you produce a more masculine rum? Well, we would start with the product, the stuff in the bottle: it would be significantly drier in taste, not as molasses-sweet as Bacardi. Then, we would make it stronger, higher in alcohol – and we arbitrarily stipulated 43%, a hefty 5% above Bacardi."

Brand Stubbs Queensland White Rum	
USP Strong (43%), dry white rum for men	
Product Made from fresh cane juice	
Client Paul Curtis, IDV marketing director	
Taste Sharp and very dry	
Ideal drinker Crocodile Dundee	
Launch 1989	
Designer Howard Waller	

The idea of white rum made from
freshly pressed cane juice sounded
so much more appetising than
thick, treacly molasses rum.

market. Was 'not invented here' at play? And even with Baileys the company's sales director was none too enthusiastic about its prospects when we first presented it.

Perhaps the bigger error was not engaging the key target market in any stage of this process: the US. All my experience in the US should have told me that you ignore these guys at your peril. They have so many tools at their disposal that will prove beyond any doubt that a brand would not sell in their market. They have distributors who will refuse it and they can devise research methods that will show clearly and absolutely that there would be no scope for an Australian high-strength dry white rum made from freshly pressed cane juice. No scope at all.

Stubbs soldiered on in the US for about three years under the stewardship of the hugely talented and committed Julie Little. I can remember her giving her sales team presentation kits showing gleaming pristine cane juice rum, Stubbs, against dark, gloopy molasses rum, Bacardi, to show the difference. But without the resources of the whole organisation behind it, our Aussie rum was never going to work. This was America.

To smart New Yorkers in the drinks business, the rest of the world was about equivalent to Montana or Honduras. Nor were Californians

Freshly pressed cane juice rum

During my reading I discovered that there were two main ways of making rum. In most cases it was made from molasses, thick, heavy, treacly stuff. But in some countries they made it with freshly pressed sugar cane juice. That seemed to fit much better with a dry, strong, 'macho' rum so we factored that into the equation as well. It was also new and different. To compete with such a powerful brand, we would need to do a 'Don Vito Corleone' and make the discerning drinker 'an offer he couldn't refuse'.

any different in that regard. I can remember reading that when Grace Kelly 'married Monaco' the top brass at MGM were happy to gift her that outstanding wedding dress, yet couldn't comprehend why she wanted to marry a European prince whose entire kingdom was smaller than their back lot.

The Americans were never really on board and so for Stubbs the music died. The Bacardi people could relax, for a while anyway. A pity, really. It was such a good idea.

I had a great blast from the past when sitting with family at a bar in Chatham on Cape Cod in the US two years ago. When I shouted "Oh my God" they thought I was going into cardiac arrest. There on the wall was a Stubbs advertising mirror. It lived. Having recovered from my excitement, I took the liberty of telling them the story, probably not for the first time.

Smirnoff Black is beautiful
Turning coal into gold?

It was now 1990 and a new group had taken over Smirnoff's global business at IDV in London and were looking for a new, premium 'super Smirnoff' to compete with two brands which were taking America by storm. These were Stolichnaya, imported from Moscow, and the stylish Absolut from Sweden.

Now this was a tough ask. At the time, Smirnoff was a pretty depressed brand in America. Serial price-cutting over the previous decade had placed it just above private label 'house' vodkas, so the idea of producing a credible 'super Smirnoff' had about as much going for it as creating a Michelin-starred restaurant under the Kentucky Fried Chicken banner. American drinkers weren't stupid. Why would they prefer a hyped-up faux Russian Smirnoff to a 'Stoli' which was the real thing?

Dennis Malamatinas, the CEO of Smirnoff, provided the first edge when he announced that the new premium vodka would be distilled and bottled in Moscow. Smirnoff would be going 'home' to its Russian roots. "Yes, but..." I thought. "...it's all very well, but Stoli has always been made in Moscow. And, despite its Menlo Park, California address, many people think that Smirnoff Red is made over there too." So being Russian wasn't going to be enough.

Coming up with an extremely stylish package wasn't going to be sufficient either. It would still be McDonalds dressed up as Le Manoir aux Quat'Saisons. Absolute improbability.

This gave rise to my first conclusion, which was going to become a leitmotif for many of my developments after that. For Smirnoff to offer a credible competitor in vodka's 'premiership' it had to offer a better product. And drinkers would need reason to believe that it was better too. If they could taste this superiority they would believe it. This would be our challenge.

Smirnoff 1818
Staring at me from the shoulder of the bottle

The answer came early, from a totally unexpected place. There it was, staring out at me, on the front of the old Smirnoff Red bottle. '1818', the date when Smirnoff was allegedly founded.

Now I won't bore you with too much technical detail but vodka, as we know it today, is made in a continuous still which was patented by the Irishman Aeneas Coffey in 1830. He was granted Patent #5974 for his design, a two-column continuous still. Given that date, original Smirnoff (born 1818) must have been made in a different kind of still, a pot still. This is the kind they use to make brown spirits like whisky and brandy. These are higher up the prestige chain than colourless, tasteless vodka.

That became the first element in the solution. To be true to Smirnoff's roots we would produce a pot-distilled vodka, made in Moscow. But pot-distillation is a process. It isn't a benefit. People can't taste it. It's a bit like those claims that products are 'triple-distilled' or 'handcrafted'. They sound good but they don't really mean a thing. If new Smirnoff was to become an effective competitor to Absolut and Stoli it needed to taste better. And ordinary drinkers needed to believe that it did. I was after a 'sale in the mouth', not a 'sale in the mind'. The latter was barely credible for Smirnoff as it was then.

As I have said repeatedly in this book, new brand development is often a question of finding a word. Once you have a word that can make your product different, you can then build it to deliver that word. The word I found was 'smooth'. If you looked at vodka vocabulary at the time (1990) the buzz words for products were 'crisp', 'clean', 'sharp', 'strong' and most commonly 'pure'. 'Smooth' was a whisky word. We had used it in creating The Singleton. It was a word that could transform a harsh, difficult spirit into a palatable one. If the product lived up to it.

Pot distillation is OK, but it's a process
What's in it for me?

And that was it. Our aim became to produce 'the smoothest-tasting vodka in the world'. If we could create a product that genuinely delivered that promise, then new Smirnoff would have a real chance of competing with the big boys.

Mac Macpherson had left IDV and retired to Cornwall but we co-opted his services to work on this as a freelance. If anyone could create a new super-smooth Smirnoff, he was the man. We travelled to New York to test our idea among hard-line Absolut and Stoli drinkers. These were cynical, seasoned neat vodka/vodka rocks drinkers. They would see through any hype or bullshit. New Smirnoff had to pass muster with these guys. There was no point in trying to kid ourselves. And we certainly couldn't kid them.

We used the magazine article device to introduce the idea to these men. It purported to be from a real publication and it articulated the idea in a bland factual way. It was presented to respondents as news rather than publicity.

The other device we used in research was a series of 'blind taste comparisons' between new Smirnoff and Absolut or Stoli. Men were given two unidentified ice-cold glasses of straight vodka to taste and

We managed, in theory at least, to convince tough New Yorkers that Smirnoff could offer perceptibly better-tasting vodka than entrenched quality premium competitors. "

were asked to rate each one, indicate their preference and articulate why they preferred one over the other. Our aim was to reach a stage where at least eight out of ten men in each group said "I prefer this one (Smirnoff) because it's smoother".

We did four focus groups (40 men in all). I conducted the sessions and Mac worked behind the scenes modifying the product after each group. Now, I won't give away Mac's secret for modifying the formula for the vodka but we were able to achieve our aim. These men really did believe that our product was smoother – and therefore better – and we managed, in theory at least, to convince tough New Yorkers that Smirnoff could offer perceptibly better-tasting vodka than entrenched quality premium competitors. Even my modest palate could tell the difference.

Dennis Malamatinas, the Smirnoff boss, fell in love with this design the first time he saw it.

Smirnoff goes home

Having been in exile since the revolution in 1917, the Smirnoff company is returning home to Moscow. To celebrate this home-coming, Smirnoff will be recruiting one of their styles of vodka originally produced for the Czars of Russia.

Known as their 'original mellow' vodka, it will be distilled and bottled in Moscow.

How does it differ from the Smirnoff we know? Their man in Moscow explained.

"Russian vodkas can vary greatly in style, and the earliest Smirnoff vodkas were made in a pot-still, the same type that they use for whiskies, even today.

While current Smirnoff is very clean and pure in taste, their original pot-still product had a little more character and 'spelya', the Russian word 'for mellowness'.

It is still remarkably pure, as we filter it through Russian silver birch charcoal, and we triple distil it, as we did for the Czar.

Moscow-made Smirnoff is available in certain markets now and is expected in the US in the spring of 1993. We shall observe its progress with interest. *Tom Halliday*

The Food Review, December 1990

The very first expression of the Smirnoff Black idea tested in focus groups in New York.

And this result was repeated a few months later when we returned to New York with Gerry Barney's brilliant pack design. In fact, drinkers were so enthusiastic about Smirnoff Black, as it became, that I had to resort to a ploy where I challenged their enthusiasm. I said in the later groups something along the lines of "You know you are the only group who really likes this idea. Other groups across the US have rejected it. They don't believe that Smirnoff can deliver premium-quality vodka". These hard-nosed New Yorkers were steadfast in their defence of new Smirnoff. They believed in the product and its story.

One of the many things I liked about this idea was the name. There wasn't one. If people came to learn about it they would find their own way of asking for it. That was confidence. And Smirnoff would need confidence to compete in this new theatre. That idea came from the client, Dennis Malamatinas. If we gave it a sexy sub-name like Smirnoff 'Alpha', for example, it would detract from the core brand name and Smirnoff would be ignored.

Smirnoff Black was created over 25 years ago. The company actually bought a small pot still in Scotland and transported it to the Cristall Distillery in Moscow. The technicians there had never seen one before and they dismantled it out of curiosity. Eventually Colin Purdey from IDV's brand development team had to come to the rescue, reassemble the still and get it up and running.

Smirnoff Black is still around after all this time, so it must have acquired a following among vodka drinkers. But I can't help feeling that IDV and then Diageo were never totally committed to the idea and preferred newer, sexier premium vodkas like Ketel One, a brand it acquired, and Cîroc (see page 212).

I think it was one of the most challenging and satisfying projects I ever worked on. And it initiated a new attitude to the development of spirit brands that would take me through to the latter part of my career. Look for the product advantage. And make it real.

Tanqueray Ten fresh botanical gin
A diamond amongst the floor sweepings

There was nothing like a request from the company CEO to inject a sense of urgency into a project. Doors opened, hurdles were set aside and things happened quickly. John McGrath, CEO of GuinnessUDV, was the instigator of this next venture.

When IDV merged with GuinnessUD in 1997 it was forced by the Monopolies & Mergers Commission to sell off two of its favourite brands, Bombay Sapphire gin and Dewar's White Label whisky. These were purchased by Bacardi in 1998 for $1.5 billion. The company was 'gin-heavy' with Gilbey's, Gordon's and Tanqueray in the merged portfolio so something had to go.

So it wasn't surprising when the brief came down from the board at GuinnessUDV, which wanted a new gin and quickly. My friend and long-time colleague, Adrian Walker, had been appointed head of the company's US innovation team and he would manage the project from the company end. We'd worked together a lot over the years and were looking forward to it. It was 1998.

Experience from Smirnoff Black led me on the path of looking for a better product –and one where gin drinkers could really taste the difference. Unlike vodka, which is pretty well tasteless and neutral, gin is a flavoured spirit and that presented an opportunity. We could engineer real differences.

The breakthrough came during a visit to the old Gordon's gin distillery in Laindon, about 30 miles east of London. Adrian and I had looked around the place and spent some time with the distillery manager, Huw Williams. We were sitting down having a break and I noticed sacks of herbs and spices all over the place. They contained the botanicals that provide the signature flavours for gin. One of the sacks was open and it contained dried juniper berries.

Instinct beats analysis every time

Despite its Victorian look and the 1761 date on the label, Bombay was a relatively modern development. It drifted into the IDV firmament in 1980, when US giant Liggett & Myers was bought. It was one of the spirit brands in their portfolio. Bombay had established a small following in the US but really hadn't set the world on fire.

Then, in 1987, the man managing the brand in the US, Michel Roux, commissioned an upgrade. He felt Bombay was capable of bigger things. The reboot of the brand was based on the featuring of a real sapphire, 'The Star of Bombay' which resides in the Smithsonian in Washington DC. That inspired the decision to put the gin into a blue bottle and from there Bombay Sapphire took off. And then the company had to let it go. It was a great pity.

Bombay Sapphire was a very attractive brand and had made gin fashionable again and carved a niche as a top-shelf super-premium product. It still enjoys that reputation today.

One of its most appealing characteristics was that it published its recipe on the bottle. Its blend of almond, lemon peel, liquorice, juniper berries, orris root, angelica, coriander, cassia, cubeb and grains of paradise gave Bombay Sapphire real appetite appeal.

And it went on to talk up the taste by saying that "The spirit is triple distilled using a carterhead still and the alcohol vapours are passed through a mesh basket containing the ten botanicals, in order to gain flavour and aroma. This gives a lighter, more floral gin rather than the more-common 'punchy' gins."

As a piece of innovation, Bombay Sapphire had a lot going for it. It flew bravely in the face of received wisdom. Consumer research would probably have pronounced that blue bottles suggest poison or at least medicine. And why Bombay? The gin wasn't from India. It was a very confident creation.

"Can you make gin out of fresh botanicals?" I idly asked Huw. I'd remembered someone cooking with fresh juniper berries and the idea of a gin made with fresh botanicals was an appetising prospect. "No problem" he replied, "but it will cost." And there, in a moment, was our idea for a new gin. It would be the world's first gin made with fresh botanicals.

But as with so many of the products I've worked on, making gin with fresh botanicals would have to be a process, leading to a story. To be convincing it would have to offer the drinker a better product – or a different product. It would have to be a gin that worked on the palate, not just in the head.

The first iteration of Tanqueray's new gin was written as a magazine article shortly after the distillery visit. We later tested the idea in New York (two focus groups, one evening) giving a product to taste that we hoped measured up to our proposition.

The solution to the product brief came from the 'dirty gin' experiment (see below). By using fresh botanicals we would set out to offer the drinker a cleaner tasting gin. Our new gin would make the

D-I-Y research: the best kind?

To get into the subject one of the first things we did was taste a whole lot of the best known gin brands. We tried them on their own and with tonic. We also tasted vodka and white rum. One of the conclusions we reached was that gin, through its mix of juniper, coriander and other herbs/spices (botanicals), had a kind of bitter, almost dirty taste.

Vodka was generally sharp and clean while rum was sweet and fuller-bodied. It didn't lead to anything immediately, but we'd made a start. And the people who tasted these gins were family and friends, not experts. We were just looking for clues. And it was a good excuse for a party.

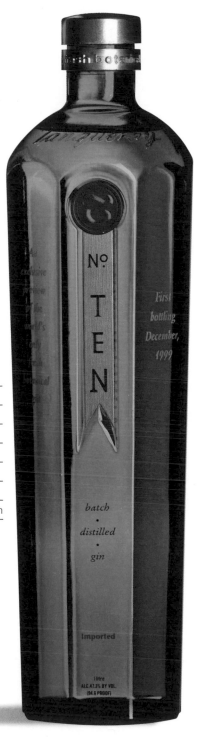

"

Making gin with fresh
botanicals would have to
be a process, leading to
a story. To be convincing
it would have to offer the
drinker a better product
– or a different product.
It would have to be a gin
that worked on the palate,
not just in the head."

Brand Tanqueray Ten

USP Fresh botanical gin

Clients John McGrath CEO and Adrian Walker

Taste Cleaner, fruitier taste than any other gin

Ideal drinker Roger Stirling's new martini

Launch 1999

Designer US Initiated, finished by Gordon Smith

Tanqueray Introduces 'Fresh Botanical Gin'

TOM GUNTHER

The London-based Tanqueray company has gone back into its archives to re-introduce a style of gin that pre-dates its famous 'London Dry'.

Their product, known as Tanqueray Classic is termed a 'fresh botanical gin'. We asked their master distiller, Huw Williams, to explain the term :

"Gin is distilled from pure grain spirit to which is added a blend of herbs, spices and fruit essences which are known as botanicals. They give the gin its distinctive flavour. The popular gins used dried botanicals like juniper and coriander, fruit peels and so on. They have become known as 'London Dry Gins'.

With Tanqueray Classic we have revived a very old recipe for gin, where we use FRESH botanicals to create the heart of our blend : fresh juniper berries from Italy, fresh coriander from Bulgaria, and fresh, not dried, fruit peel.

The result is a very distinctive gin taste. The character of the fresh juniper and coriander are clearly in evidence and this is beautifully balanced with the fragrant fruitiness of the other botanicals. Classic is both fresh and dry with a distinctive underlying character.

Its taste comes through even when its served straight from the freezer and it provides the base for a very distinctive martini. It is also robust enough to shine through in a gin and tonic.

Tanqueray Classic is currently produced in small batches and is available locally in select bars. It is priced at about $20 a bottle.

The very first representation of Tanqueray Ten tested in New York. Here we called it Tanqueray Classic. Ten came later.

best martini in the world. (It still does.) We would coin a new gin word. Fresh. That was our brief to the liquid developers. And, despite Adrian's new elevated status as head of innovation in the US, he became very hands-on in producing the liquid.

The next issue was to decide on the brand. Do we go with an extension of an existing brand, a super Gordon's or Tanqueray gin, or do we develop a new brand from scratch? Companies generally prefer to go with existing brands. They have been around a long time, received huge investment and people know them: retailers, bartenders and consumers. Both Gordon's and Gilbey's were locally-produced (in the US) domestic gins and much lower down the 'food chain' even than Smirnoff. They were not real candidates for a 'super gin'. Tanqueray, made in the UK, with its distinctive 'fire hydrant' bottle shape was by far the most promising option.

Tanqueray was an 'OK' gin but nothing special. It was middle-aged, white collar and conservative but with nothing like the charisma of Bombay Sapphire. It would need a real product edge to compete. We thought we had it. We would recommend Tanqueray Fresh Botanical Gin.

We settled on the sub-name Tanqueray Ten, and it was introduced into the US in 2000. The beautiful bottle was developed in the US and refined by UK designer Gordon Smith. The botanicals were distilled in a small pot-still in the Laindon distillery. It was the tenth and smallest in a row of stills and we christened it 'Tiny Ten' – hence the name.

While it has not yet knocked Bombay Sapphire off its pedestal, it has become a respectable member of Diageo's premium brand portfolio.

In hindsight, the most disappointing aspect of this creation – for me anyway – has been the lack of interest in communicating the 'fresh botanicals = fresh taste' idea. Advertising people prefer emotional fantasies to product stories. I genuinely believe that if you have a product that really tastes different, and better for some, you should make that the cornerstone of your brand story. People will try it. And if they like it, they'll buy it again. You can save the emotional sell until everybody gets the message.

The birthplace of Cîroc
Georgia on my mind

If you visit New York and ask about the hottest vodka in town, you'll get two names, Cîroc and the name of its advocate and promoter, the rapper P. Diddy. What you may not discover is that the seed for the idea germinated in the most unlikely location on the other side of the world – in faraway Georgia, part of the old Soviet Union. It was the home of Eduard Shevardnadze and, more famously, Iosif Vissarionovich Dzhugashvili – better known as Joseph Stalin.

The time was 1995, the place Tbilisi. Adrian Walker, who was then managing Smirnoff's global business from the UK, and I were on a fact-finding mission looking for new vodka ideas for Smirnoff. We were hoping to discover products from the old Soviet Union, possibly to offer as a range of regional vodkas under the Smirnoff banner. Our trip took in Kiev in the Ukraine and Tbilisi in Georgia.

We came up with a number of ideas but one, first unearthed in the Sarajishvili brandy distillery in the centre of Tbilisi, was to take a series of unexpected turns on the road to fortune for the company a decade later.

I can remember the dialogue as if it were yesterday. Adrian and I had been dragooned into doing a distillery tour of Sarajishvili even though brandy was nowhere in our minds. Our host was desperate to show us the distillery. It was Stalin's favourite and there are pictures of him and Winston Churchill enjoying cigars and Sarajishvili's premier brandy. Adrian had a technical background so would have found some items of interest in the tour. My eyes glazed over at the thought of yet another distillery visit. I am not technical and boredom invariably set in after about half an hour.

During the trudge around I noticed a plaque showing the foundation date of the distillery as 1884 and decided to engage our guide in polite conversation giving some pretence of civility: "Was this the first brandy distillery in Georgia?" Having received a "yes" answer I went on to ask whether this was the first time brandy was made in Georgia. Again, an affirmative answer.

"OK, if that's the case, then what did Georgians drink before brandy?" I asked. "Vodka" was the immediate reply, "We call it Cha-cha." That really puzzled me. Tblisi is quite far south, on similar latitude to Barcelona, Naples and Athens, and far from the great Soviet grain basket of the Ukraine. I thought we might be on to something and continued.

"And what did you use to make this vodka?" "Grapes" was the reply, "Cha-cha is grape vodka". And that was it. It wasn't a formal category but rather a product made by local farmers, a kind of 'Georgia moonshine'. This brief interchange became the basis for a new style of vodka and we developed, as an idea only, Smirnoff Georgian grape vodka. There was nothing in the vodka regulations that said you couldn't make grape vodka. It just had to be 'tasteless, colourless and odourless...'

The idea was never taken further and we put it away for eight years.

Peel me a grape
Dancing to a Cha-cha beat

Fast forward to 2003. Diageo had become the biggest alcoholic
beverage company in the known universe. It was an amalgam of
IDV (J&B, Baileys, Smirnoff, Gilbey's, Jose Cuervo), United Distillers
Guinness (Johnnie Walker, Gordon's, Tanqueray, Bell's, Guinness)
and most recently Seagram's (Captain Morgan, Crown Royal). If there
was somewhere in the market where it was not represented, it had the
muscle to change that.

Adrian Walker was by this time in the US in charge of Diageo's
innovation team. Tanqueray Ten was up and running but the company
was concerned with the rapid growth of a new super-premium vodka
from France called Grey Goose.

Grey Goose was taking the US by storm. It was the brainchild of
one of the great innovators in the US liquor market, Sidney Frank,
the man who had built Jägermeister into a huge success. Our mission,
which came from on high, was to create a new vodka to compete with
Grey Goose. Adrian had had a good start with Tanqueray Ten. But this
was an altogether tougher challenge. Remember that vodka has to be
odourless, flavourless and colourless. Not like gin with all its herbs,
spices, fruits and botanicals.

Adrian and I met in London and came to a conclusion similar to the
one we had reached with Tanqueray and Smirnoff Black. We must look
to develop a genuinely new, different vodka. Let's offer the up-market
vodka enthusiast a functionally differentiated product. Let's create a
product that can tell a better story than Grey Goose. It could be done.

It didn't take too long. We dug into our intellectual archive and were
soon back in Tbilisi, being taken around Sarjashvili learning about
brandy and discovering Cha-cha. That was it. We'd do the Cha-cha –
the grape vodka, not the dance. There was nothing in the US vodka

"

By 2014 Cîroc had become one of the hottest drinks brands in the US, with sales in excess of three million cases. It is even known on the street as 'Diddy Juice'."

Brand Cîroc, made from snap-frost grapes

USP The world's first grape vodka brand

Client Adrian Walker, Diageo USA

Taste Dry, sophisticated, great martini vodka

Ideal drinker Sean Combs aka P Diddy

Launch 2002

Designer Gordon Smith, Smith & Co

regulations that said you couldn't make vodka out of grapes.

I was also intrigued by the popular belief, in the UK at least, that you 'shouldn't mix grain and grape'. Doing so would give you a terrible hangover. With more and more people drinking wine these days, would grape vodka make a more compatible cocktail if you were going to move to wine later on in the evening? As it turned out this piece of folk wisdom had no currency in the US. People looked blankly at me when I mentioned it. Aside from doing a few focus groups in New York to check out the idea alongside a few other 'benchmark' ideas, my personal involvement in this venture came to an early end. The US company wanted to pass the project on to local consultants so that it could exercise closer control. That decision appears to have been justified as

Memories of a meister

Though I never met him, Sidney Frank was one of my heroes. He had a great instinct for the business and he really had balls. Drinking Jägermeister, an exceptionally bitter German herbal liqueur, was a punishing assignment. But Frank believed in it and set up a team of beautiful young women, the 'Jägerettes', who went around US college campuses sampling the product and spreading the word. It took patience and it took time. But Sidney wasn't going anywhere.

Founded in Germany in 1935, Jägermeister was nicknamed Leberkleister (liver glue) and it is ironic that Sidney Frank, chief benefactor to the Israel Olympic committee, should make his first fortune from a drink also known as 'Göring-schnapps' after Hitler's close associate and one of the founders of the Nazi party.

When he introduced Grey Goose, Frank showed the same chutzpah. He created a new price level, above Absolut, Stolichnaya and Smirnoff Black. His new vodka wasn't just premium. Or even super-premium. It was ultra Premium.

the brand has become extremely successful. It was named Cîroc and Adrian used Gordon Smith, the designer who worked on Tanqueray Ten, to produce a stunning pack design.

The company also followed the Grey Goose route and sourced the product from France. And Adrian's technical expertise added a further refinement, basing the vodka on snap-frost grapes, the kind of grapes used to make the famous Eiswein.

Cîroc started promisingly in the US and won plenty of plaudits from top 'foodies', especially in metro areas like Boston and New York. But it received its real momentum through a stroke of marketing genius by someone at Diageo. In 2007 it negotiated a deal with famous US rapper Sean Combs, otherwise known as P. Diddy. He would use his marketing muscle to promote it in the US. And that he did.

By 2014 Cîroc had become one of the hottest drinks in the US, with sales in excess of three million cases. It is even known on the street as 'Diddy Juice'. It's all a long, long way from that jet-lagged morning traipsing unenthusiastically around Sarjashvili distillery in Tbilisi.

Chapter Eight
Bits and pieces

I worked as a product developer for IDV/ Diageo from 1969–2005. It was an astonishing amount of time to spend working as an outside consultant to a single company. It was a privilege and a pleasure.

As we've seen from the earlier pages, not every idea worked or was taken up by companies within the network. Or some rose, shone briefly, and then faded into oblivion. Successes or failures, I loved them all. It was fantastic seeing something that started off in your own head being brought to life by a stunning design or a superbly crafted liquid.

I have included here the best of these ideas. Most didn't make it. Some flourished for a while. All but one, Sheridan's, is now defunct but each has a story worth telling. Who knows, someone may think of reviving one or two of them at some time in the future.

Raffles Singapore Sling
"Ours was better"

One of the earliest briefs we received, even before Baileys, was to develop a Gin Sling mix for Gilbeys Canada. It was a project 'to encourage the troops' rather than a serious undertaking – as we later discovered. Hunting through libraries in that pre-internet era, we discovered that the Gin Sling had been created in the bar at the famous Raffles hotel in Singapore. Bob Wagner got onto the case and created a wonderfully atmospheric label evoking all the feel of its location. Legal, however, said we couldn't show Sir Stamford Raffles on the label – so we settled for Tom Jago, who looked great. Sadly, the Canadians managed not to run with the idea.

Mac Macpherson and his team did a wonderful job on the liquid which had a rich and full-bodied cherry brandy taste with an underlying juniper hit. Topped up with lemonade or soda, shaved ice and a sprig of mint as a garnish, Raffles really showed how good the IDV technical people were with liquids. I loved the brand – it was one of my first and I was sad to see it disappear.

Fifteen years on, Mac Macpherson and I had the opportunity to stay at Raffles. It was the 'pre-designer' version, shabby but with loads of character. We sat in the garden listening to an out-of-tune brass band, sipping the real thing – a Raffles Singapore Sling in a plastic glass. We looked at each other and agreed – ours was better.

The British Empire on a label, with Tom standing in for Sir Stamford Raffles.

Primavera
Miracle marmalade

One of the hottest brands in the UK in the early seventies was the Italian aperitif Martini Rosso. The ads showed beautiful people in beautiful places doing exciting things – skiing, Grand Prix, ballooning – with uptempo modern music and the lyric: "Anytime, anyplace, anywhere... There's a wonderful world we can share... It's the bright one... It's the right one... That's Martini".

Fairly new in the business, we could only sit and watch Tom Jago's courageous genius and Mac Macpherson's 'can do' approach to all things technical. Our reply to Martini was a bitter orange aperitif called Primavera. Tom had the inspired idea of suggesting a marmalade taste. It was adult, it was distinctive and it just worked. And we also discovered that the most effective way of achieving this was to pump vast quantities of real marmalade into the IDV plant in Harlow. We were always in a hurry and that was the only way we could guarantee getting the taste we were after quickly.

Primavera was a delicious product that built up a cult following in the UK. But it failed to set the world on fire or shake the boys at Martini so it was pulled after about five years. If someone at Diageo has access to the original recipe, it would be well worth resurrecting for a vodka or gin product. (I notice that the Chase vodka people have a marmalade vodka and, good as it is, it doesn't hold a candle to Primavera.)

I should add that although party to the original idea – we wanted to call it Miura (the bull) after Lamborghini – Tom's boss co-opted an ad agency to brand it, so they created the name and label design.

"

Tom had the inspired idea of suggesting a marmalade taste. It was adult, it was distinctive and it just worked. And we also discovered that the most effective way of achieving this was to pump vast quantities of real marmalade into the IDV factory in Harlow."

Brand Primavera

USP Unique bitter orange taste

Client Tom Jago, IDV

Taste Marmalade with sherry undertones

Ideal drinker Modesty Blaise

Launch Circa 1972

Designer Unknown

Howard Waller's brilliant poster inspired by Cuban cigar box design.

St Leger
Britain's first alcopop

Although I had ventured into the beer business on several occasions, IDV and its wine and spirits remained my first love. We were beset with the problem: 'How can we find a product that can be as frequently purchased as beer? How can we develop an everyday alcoholic drink?'

By now we were in the early eighties and times were changing. Unlikely drinks like Perrier were taking off. Sparkling mineral water from France was selling at the same price as newly arriving imported lagers. People were moving from spirits such as gin and tonic to wine and some from wine to wine spritzers. They were thinking healthier and acting it too. Sports club membership was on the up and phrases like 'healthy lifestyle' were striding confidently into the language.

And this wasn't only happening in the UK. Perrier was also a sensation in the US. The UK 'eau' advertising – perhaps too French for America – was one of the most memorable beverage campaigns in my time.

The question now became 'how could we take advantage of these healthy trends to create a unique new beverage that people would want to drink as often as beer?'

The formula presented itself quite quickly and it went something like this: what worked for beer was that it was relatively low in alcohol (4–5%) versus wine (about 12%) or spirits (40%). And because it was low in alcohol, you could drink it in larger quantities, pints and half pints. It was a quaffing drink for quenching the thirst, not a sipping drink like wine or gin and tonic. (If this all sounds obvious, it's because it was. This was simple common sense with not an astrophysicist or behavioural psychologist in sight.)

Another conclusion that fed into the equation was that there was a large body of people, usually women, who were not enchanted with beer, neither English bitter nor sweeter, blander lagers. I can recall doing focus groups with women when some expressed the thought that they detested the very idea of a glass of fizzy, foaming brown liquid. They loathed the smell, they hated the taste and they simply did not like the very idea of even associating themselves with a glass of beer sitting in front of them in a public place. It just didn't look right.

The first of our building blocks was wine: that would provide the alcohol base. And we chose a dry white wine. It was contemporary, sophisticated and less fattening than beer. Then we took a leaf out of the Perrier manual and added sparkling spring water. And the final link in the chain was orange juice, by far the most popular of the fruit juice varieties. We felt it all added up to a tastier, healthier, more interesting drink which would have a real chance of creaming off some beer business.

Mac Macpherson and his team spent a lot of time on the product and we all drank gallons of it during the development phases until we were pretty confident that we had an attractive liquid. The next stage was to brand it and design the bottle.

On this occasion we again worked with the brilliant, volatile Howard Waller. We started with the bottle. He created a beautiful half-pint unit that had some of the curves of a Perrier bottle. We used a simple research technique to decide on bottle colour. It took ten minutes and cost pennies. Our product was predominantly orange so we went out and bought some available bottles in flint (clear), brown and green glass. We filled each one with orange juice and drew some conclusions: in clear it looked like orange juice – and that would make it look cheap. In a brown glass the orange product looked brown, like Baileys, while in green it looked like the late lamented Greensleeves – the green creamy liquid described in Chapter 2.

So we chose to go with a black bottle.

Still obsessed with the beer connection, we originally named the brand Prost (meaning 'good luck' or 'cheers' in German) to give it a kind of continental lager feel. We thought that a few people would be familiar with the term and the French motor racing driver Alain Prost added further respectability to it.

But the Prost brand name died the death after a single comment by a young lady in a focus group, in fact the last group that we did. Up until that point, nobody had commented on the name and people seemed comfortable using it. But this woman said "I can't imagine going up to a bar and asking for a bottle of Prost. It reminds me of prostitutes

This woman said 'I can't imagine going up to a bar and asking for a bottle of Prost. It reminds me of prostitutes or prostates'. She was absolutely right and we knew exactly what she meant. We dumped the name immediately."

or prostates". She was absolutely right and we knew exactly what she meant. We dumped the name immediately. Tom called a couple of days later and said "Let's call it St Leger." There was no explanation and no justification but it was fine with me.

The other thing we did was to avoid giving St Leger a designation such as 'wine cooler' or 'fruit spritzer'. If we had done that, we would have created a category – and that would have made it easier for people to copy. So we settled on telling people what was in the bottle: sparkling spring water, pure orange juice and dry white wine. Waller had the inspired idea that we translate the copy into French, Italian and German so that St Leger would start life looking like an internationally famous drink. He based part of the theme on an antique cigar box and the graphics for the bottle and the six-pack were really striking. And, painstaking craftsman that he was, he drew every single line of the artwork himself.

St Leger came and went in the UK only. It even had a TV commercial to support it. We were unable to persuade any of the other companies in the group to join us. And although IDV was in the same corporate stable as the brewers Watneys, it didn't manage to persuade that company to take on distribution for St Leger. It was clearly 'not invented there'.

One big mistake that we made was going with an orange liquid. It looked too much like a soft drink even though the black bottle obscured that on the shelf. Later brands like Smirnoff Ice went with a more sophisticated-looking cloudy lemon product and that, together with the endorsement of an internationally famous vodka brand, resulted in far greater success. And interestingly, at around the same time as we were working on St Leger, a US brand, California Cooler, exploded onto the market. It was chasing exactly the same objective as we were. And it was a cloudy green liquid.

These 'coolers' or 'RTDs' (ready-to-drinks) came in phases into the drinks market. California Cooler and St Leger started things off in the mid-eighties and, in the US especially, there were a host of imitators. Then an Australian product called Two Dogs, billed as brewed alcoholic lemonade, brought the category to life again in the nineties and spawned imitators like Hooper's Hooch and others.

The most recent foray into this sector was the enormously successful Smirnoff Ice which reached record-breaking volumes in the late 1990s and early 2000s.

Interestingly, all these drinks were going after the same piece of pie in the market. They all wanted some beer business. And each time a brand was launched and was really successful – California Cooler, Two Dogs, Smirnoff Ice – it attracted enormous competition, the market soared to dizzy heights and then imploded.

Maybe there is a limit to how many of these sweet-tasting, multi-flavoured drinks the consumer can take. Fatigue sets in and they go back to drinking beer. Perhaps for products to be eternally successful like beer, whisky, brandy et al, they need to be 'difficult to like' and need time for us to acquire a taste for them. This rite of passage may be really important.

In today's market research-dominated business environment, it is becoming increasingly difficult for tough, complex products to make their way. Some do, of course, and the most recent notable success has been Jägermeister, the German bitter liqueur. But how many companies in the future will have the cojones to go with products that are not immediately palatable to more than a small percentage of atypical consumers? Imagine putting whisky into a focus group for the very first time and expecting a majority of people to take an immediate liking to it. No chance.

Carignac from Bordeaux
Better than Cognac?

Fear and panic are great stimuli in the creative process. It's Sunday night at 11pm, you have a meeting at 9am next morning and you're desperate to find something to contribute. It conjures up the saying attributed to Dr Johnson that: "The prospect of being hanged focuses the mind wonderfully". Well, it wasn't quite as serious as that, but you know what I mean.

The brief was to come up with some new thinking about brandy. The cognac category was pretty well sewn up. IDV didn't own one so could we do something with humble old brandy which would take it to a new level?

I sat down at the typewriter and looked around my kitchen. You have to be an optimist in this job and I somehow knew that something would turn up. And it did. There in the room was an empty wine bottle. On the label was the word 'Bordeaux' and then everything clicked. An idea began to form.

If you think about it, cognac comes from a particular region in France. And almost everything about food and drink in France is about region and appellation contrôlée. The French are very skilled at cordoning off an area of their country and making it special, which

"

The best wine in the world comes from Bordeaux. Wine is made from grapes. Brandy is made from grapes. Therefore Bordeaux grapes would make the best brandy."

Brand Carignac Liqueur Brandy

USP Classier than Cognac or Armagnac

Client Patrick Copeland, IDV marketing director

Taste Richer and mellower than Cognac

Ideal drinker Jean-Paul Belmondo

Launch Never

Designer Howard Waller, Sedley Place

means making its produce more expensive. They do it with cheese, with ham, with chickens – Poulet de Bresse – and even eggs, from Marans. Then there is wine, of course, champagne and brandy, hence Cognac. Developing this theme, I asked myself the question: 'What happens if we create a new region for brandy?'

A syllogism began to write itself. "The best wine in the world comes from Bordeaux. Wine is made from grapes. Brandy is made from grapes. Therefore Bordeaux grapes would make the best brandy." That may not necessarily be true, but it sounds pretty good. And IDV had the technical skills to make the product deliver the promise.

Why not Bordeaux brandy? I managed to sell the idea and Mac went to Bordeaux to commission a product. We called it Carignac which is a name we stole from a South African IDV product which never happened. Waller did yet another great pack. But we couldn't get anyone to take it seriously. IDV's people wanted a Cognac. This was interfering with nature. But it wasn't a bad outcome from looking at a wine bottle on a Sunday night.

Oxford Blue
English summertime in a bottle

We managed to 'recycle' the lovely Primavera marmalade taste (see page 224) in a product developed fifteen years later in 1985 for the Gilbey's gin team. They wanted a mid-strength white spirit product for the UK and Europe. It should be about 24% alcohol, like Malibu – these mid-proof drinks were catching on – and we used the original Primavera bottle mould.

Designer Kit Cooper produced a wonderful label based on the famous Farrah's Harrogate Toffee packaging. We called the product Gilbey's Oxford Blue and the atmosphere we tried to conjure up was that of England in high summer at the peak of the 'season': Royal Ascot, Lord's cricket ground, Wimbledon, Henley Regatta, Glyndebourne.

Oxford Blue was tested in pubs and liquor stores in the Henley area but we couldn't get anyone too excited about it. We saw it as a kind of 'Pimm's-buster' but it didn't happen. Sometimes ideas need time to take root and attention spans in the company were getting shorter. And as it turned out over a decade later, Pimm's entered the company stable when IDV merged with GuinnessUD in 1997.

"

The atmosphere we tried to conjure up was that of England in high summer at the peak of the 'season': Royal Ascot, Lord's cricket ground, Wimbledon, Henley Regatta, Glyndebourne."

Brand Gilbey's Oxford Blue

USP English summer in a bottle

Client Aidan Jenkins, IDV UK

Taste Light marmalade gin

Ideal drinker Sebastian Flyte

Launch 1987

Designer Kit Cooper, Sedley Place

Water-borne revellers enjoying the season at Henley in 1908. A little Mozart after the Diamond Sculls.

This illustration beautifully represented an alcoholic
drink that looked good enough to eat.

Abercrombie's Prairie Dog
Better than a Bloody Mary

Every so often someone would come up with a brief for a savoury alcoholic drink. (Heston Blumenthal hadn't been invented yet.) I'd once come across an Italian drink based on artichokes called Cynar but that didn't taste too savoury. What were they after: a chopped liver cordial perhaps?

The idea came from an unlikely source. It started with the brand name and the rest was built from there.

When working on these jobs you never really stop thinking. In the bath, shaving, lying in bed, you were always mulling over the latest brief. This time I was doing the *Times* crossword on a Saturday morning. Most of it was done but there was a big clue as yet unfinished. It looked like this P-A-R-E S-H-O-E- and the clue was something like "covered wagon (7,8)". I dug into the dictionary and unearthed 'Prairie Schooner', the answer, but there alongside it was another phrase which became the basis for our savoury alcoholic drink. It was Prairie Dog.

I loved the sound of it and it conjured up the idea of a 'Prairie Oyster', that blend of raw egg, Worcester sauce and Tabasco that is used as a morning-after drink. It was easy to imagine going up to a bar and asking for a 'Prairie Dog'. Sounded like a good call. These things are often about instinct. Prairie Dog just felt right. And on the canine theme, I discovered that there was a drink called 'Salty Dog'. But despite the name, this was sweet not savoury.

Once the door had been opened the rest of the idea took on a life of its own. The drink became Abercrombie's Prairie Dog, long before Abercrombie & Fitch had its rebirth, and the legend I dreamed up was that of a drink created by Scottish engineers working on the trans-Peruvian railway. They drank it during the heat of the day to restore salt to their bodies. Well, this was pure hokum which we would never try to pass off as true, but it explained the idea to everyone who worked on it, product people and designers. They didn't disappoint.

There was another call for design-Waller and he gave it his best, as always. We went for a small bottle, 100ml – a bit like a Tabasco bottle – and Mac and his team produced a delicious product. It was based on dry sherry rather than spirit – we wanted to keep alcohol duty low – and it contained vegetable juices, hot chilli spices and, the pièce de résistance, oyster sauce. Perhaps this was inspired by 'Prairie Oyster'. It tasted terrific.

And the packaging was really striking too. The graphics were rich with a bit of subtle wit too – a cartoon of a man in a small fishing boat, his line dangling in the water. The caption read: 'Time for a bite'. Howard also came up with the cheeky line 'Better than a Bloody Mary'. He argued that we needed to give potential consumers some idea as to what was in the bottle.

We tested Prairie Dog in Cambridge as we thought it might go down well with students. I remember developing a series of beer mats entitled 'Eccentric Moments in Sport' adapting Edwardian cartoons from Punch. We hoped that it would be used as a kind of change-of-pace drink during a beer session – the liquid equivalent of a packet of spicy crisps.

The 'juice' was wonderful, spicy on top with a lovely complex array of flavours swirling beneath: tomato, smoked oyster, chilli and sherry. It really was 'Better than a Bloody Mary'. Much better. I can almost taste it now.

Maybe there were now too many innovative pioneering brands in the IDV system. We gave Prairie Dog about a year in Cambridge and then it was pulled. I guess it wasn't everybody's cup of tea and I can remember an American member of IDV saying "How can you name a drink after a filthy, dirty animal like that?" Well it takes all sorts and Mac and I still love the memory of our beloved dead dog.

LADY Millicent Forbes-Macindo in an illegal attempt to win the 1908 Olympic Standing Long Jump. The dog was considered an unfair advantage.

ABERCROMBIE'S ORIGINAL 'PRAIRIE DOG'
ECCENTRIC MOMENTS IN SPORT
Nº 1

Eccentric Prairie Dog beer mats based on Edwardian cartoons.

WILBERFORCE-Carruthers, a true sport, disdains the use of firearms as he prepares to wrestle a charging rhinoceros with his bare hands.

ABERCROMBIE'S ORIGINAL 'PRAIRIE DOG'
ECCENTRIC MOMENTS IN SPORT
Nº 2

LORD Hetherington visiting his psycho-analyst before contesting the 1919 Men's Singles Final.

ABERCROMBIE'S ORIGINAL 'PRAIRIE DOG'
ECCENTRIC MOMENTS IN SPORT
Nº 5

ENGLAND versus Ireland in an early eliminator for the America's Cup.

ABERCROMBIE'S ORIGINAL 'PRAIRIE DOG'
ECCENTRIC MOMENTS IN SPORT
Nº 4

Belle-Marie
Canadian capers

This is another one of those drinks ideas that didn't get too far. It was commissioned by a man called Denis Carisse from IDV's Canadian company. Like Deepak Roy from India, Denis was teetotal. But it didn't stop him commissioning a new brand. I thought initially that it was another 'sow's ear' brief but we had to make the best of it.

Denis said that Canada produced the best blueberries in the world and he wanted to introduce a blueberry liqueur. On first acquaintance I hated the idea. Blueberries to me meant pancakes and breakfast. Or at best blueberry was part of a cheap product range, one of a dozen flavours. I pictured a dark, reddish-brown sweet, sickly liquid. How can you take a picture like that and make it special?

To me the word 'blueberry' sounded cheap and easy to copy. So source the product from Montreal in French Canada and call it 'myrtilles'. That sounds a whole lot classier than pancake fodder.

Then there seemed little promise in a sweet, sticky, dark liqueur. It would get lost in the crowd of cheap local brands. Let's produce a blueberry-flavoured mid-strength white spirit. It would be akin to light blueberry vodka.

I very much enjoyed the naming of this product. My first thought about Canada was Mounties, the Royal Canadian mounted police. They represented an archetypal Canadian image like cuckoo clocks for Switzerland. There was something Monty Python about Mounties but that distinctive uniform, especially the famous 'Campaign' hat, was about as Canadian as you can get. Mounties reminded me of the 1930s operetta with Jeanette MacDonald and Nelson Eddy called *Rose Marie*.

We couldn't really call the drink 'Rose Marie'. The name was too feminine and the operetta connection wasn't exactly smart and contemporary. But I felt that I was hot on the trail. As with so many

"

The suggested name was
Belle-Marie – 'lovely Mary'
as opposed to 'Bloody
Mary'. It just felt right."

Brand Belle-Marie

USP French Canada in a glass

Client Denis Carisse, Gilbeys Canada

Taste Light blueberry vodka

Ideal drinker Modern art lovers

Launch Never

Designer Howard Waller

Illustrator Pete Denmark

other ventures, the solution just popped out. As I've said before, finding a name was one of the toughest challenges. This was no exception. The suggested name was Belle-Marie – 'lovely Mary' as opposed to 'Bloody Mary'. It just felt right. And I managed to persuade Denis, Mac and the rest of the gang to accept it too.

Then Waller got to work on the package and produced an intriguing modern design based on artwork by his friend the artist Pete Denmark, like Howard sadly now deceased. The drink itself tasted very good, sharp and subtle, and the bottle was a real 'one-off'. We tested it in the US, in Florida, and one of the subjects I raised was what Americans thought of their Canadian neighbours. The responses were intriguing: "plodding people", "poor tippers" and "terrible drivers" were some of the comments. Canada didn't offer a thrilling provenance for a new drink.

The Belle-Marie offering went down moderately well, but not well enough. It never ventured beyond the drawing board.

Sullivans 'Country Still'
The other Irish company also wanted a Baileys

In the early eighties, once Baileys was up and running as a world brand, we were approached by Trevor McLintock, who ran IDV's Northern Irish company. He too wanted a brand of his own, another Baileys if possible. We proposed a spirit based on Northern Ireland's famous Armagh apples and gave the package a homespun rustic look. Then we thought that it would be interesting to package it in a tin container so that it looked aged and authentic. We approached the Metal Box company to help us achieve this. They offered us the help of their in-house design department who produced the beautiful label shown on the opposite page.

We discovered that there were technical problems at the time and that high-strength spirit might have a corrosive effect on the inside of

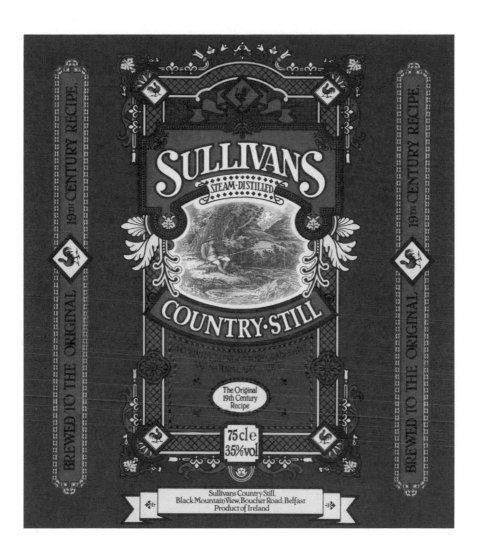

Belfast's answer to Baileys, ably designed by Metal Box.

the tin. Our compromise was to create a metal sleeve that encased the main body of the bottle. It was a good product but never managed to get off the ground.

Sheridan's
Dublin airport inspiration

It was the mid-1980s and the cream liqueur business was booming. Baileys was blazing the trail while look-alikes were appearing across the globe. Even the famous Dublin coffee house, Bewley's, had entered the fray with a coffee cream liqueur of its own. Baileys became really concerned as the coffee house was a long-established Dublin institution. It was a 'must visit' location for visitors to the city. The company saw this as a threat and wanted to riposte with a coffee liqueur of its own. I feared this was another 'poisoned' brief. A lot of people thought that Baileys had some coffee in it anyway while others would occasionally add a shot to their after-dinner coffee. Why did we need a coffee-flavoured Baileys? Or a coffee liqueur from Baileys? It would deflect attention from 'the real thing'. But that was the brief and a good strong solution was required.

It was close to Christmas and we agreed with the Baileys people that we would meet at a hotel alongside Dublin airport so we could complete our discussions by early afternoon. My flight got in at 9am and on arrival I went to the bar to buy some matches. The barman was pouring a pint of Guinness and even this early in the morning it looked utterly captivating. It started out chocolate-coloured, like a giant Baileys, and then the colours separated to create that wonderful black and white phenomenon. Gorgeous.

By 10am everyone had assembled in our suite and the Baileys team was preparing to deliver a presentation on global coffee liqueur sales trends as part of the new product brief. The company had changed a bit

The inspiring sight of a
meticulously poured pint
of Guinness – beautiful.

It started out chocolate-coloured, like a giant Baileys, and then the colours separated to create that wonderful black and white phenomenon. Gorgeous."

Brand Sheridan's

USP Unique double bottle

Client Pat Rigney, Baileys

Taste Sip the coffee through the cream

Ideal drinker Whitney Houston

Launch 1988

Designer Howard Waller

since 1974. The bluff, amiable 'Wexford Whisper' types had given way to smart, sophisticated new-age marketing people. The project brief was a massive tome of market figures and consumer trends.

I interrupted proceedings to ask for a pint of Guinness. I explained that I'd had a heavy night and needed restoration. Pat Rigney, head of the client contingent, seemed to think it a bit excessive but after some good-natured pre-Christmas banter he agreed and I called down to room service. On came the coffee sales charts.

The pint soon appeared and there followed probably the quickest presentation of a new idea I ever did. It was delivered even before we'd received the brief. I was accompanied by Alan Wilton and Colin Purdey from IDV's technical group.

I held up the pint and said "How would you like a coffee cream liqueur where you drink the coffee (pointing to the dark part of the Guinness) through the cream (the white part)? I am sure we can do it." In my excitement I dredged up a recollection of those old-fashioned liqueur bottles from the 1940s where you had as many as four different products in the same four-compartment bottle, each with its own cork. I could imagine packaging along those lines. In fact I'd recently seen such a bottle in the reception at Fonseca, a winery in Portugal owned by IDV.

The idea was to offer a double bottle with 10 per cent white creamy liquid and 90 per cent black coffee liqueur. When poured together, the dark part would escape quickly and settle at the bottom of the glass, while the white part would float gently on top. It would look like a miniature pint of Guinness or an Irish coffee – with a touch of theatre. That was the theory.

The result was surprising. Pat and his team bought the idea there and then, there were no more boring charts and we headed into town for an early lunch. It was a thrilling encounter and took a fraction of the time devoted to the Baileys pitch. By holding up the pint and showing exactly how the product would appear, I made the sale.

There was a directive to move quickly and we put the idea into focus groups straight after Christmas. Our provisional name was Dubliner and we faked the product by using an existing coffee liqueur (might have been Kenya Gold) coloured to look like Guinness. We used aerosol fresh cream for the white part. It was love at first sight (and taste) for the people we interviewed.

Mind you, I think everyone was so committed to the idea that we would have gone ahead whatever the research result. Though nearly 15 years since Baileys started, everyone remembered its moderate research performance.

The brand emerged as Sheridan's. The pack was another stunning Howard Waller original and now, nearly 30 years on, it is a respectable though not earth-shattering member of Diageo's brand portfolio. And it all came from 30 seconds at the bar in Dublin airport.

There was a slight altercation about the name of this one. I had come up with the idea of calling it Dove & Bourne which would abbreviate to D&B and imagined a beautifully antiqued label with a dove flying over a stream. I think it was inspired by Crabtree & Evelyn's crab apple tree.

But why Dove & Bourne you may ask? Well the 'dove' was from the Irish word 'dub' (as in 'Dublin'). It means 'black' and Dublin translates to mean 'black pool'. Illuminating? And 'bourne' was a variation on 'ban', the Irish word for 'white'. Perhaps it was a bit too tortuous and over-intellectualised and they settled for Sheridan's.

Godet
Belgian white chocolate – with attitude

The Baileys people issued two seemingly ridiculous briefs in 12 months: following Sheridans we received a request for a 'chocolate cream liqueur' during the latter part of 1987.

Why would they want to do that, I thought? It seemed like a crazy idea. Remember when we did Baileys back in 1973? We called it a 'chocolate cream liqueur'. Even our homemade prototype was based on Cadbury's Drinking Chocolate. And if Baileys tasted of anything, it tasted of chocolate. Why do it?

Despite the protest the word was to "get on with it". The directive from IDV's management was that we had to provide a positive response to every brief, no matter how uncomfortable or bizarre it seemed to be.

Ideas come in the strangest ways, often when you least expect them. I was heading to IDV's offices at York Gate, off London's Regent's Park, and riding the up escalator at Baker Street station. It was a week before Christmas and the station was festooned with gift ads for Marks & Spencer. They were running an 'alphabet' poster campaign and there, on the wall, was a big 'B' FOR BELGIAN CHOCOLATE poster.

And at that moment the door opened to a chocolate liqueur with a difference. We would do a white Belgian chocolate cream liqueur. And we would base it on Cognac, not Irish whiskey. That way we would keep it as far away from Baileys as possible. And we'd even price it well above Baileys to create a new premium sector of the market.

IDV had recently acquired the Metaxa Greek brandy company and in the 'suitcase' we discovered a tiny Cognac brand from La Rochelle in France called Godet. It had been around since 1838 and would provide the perfect underpinning for our new premium product. And, as usual, designer Howard Waller delivered a fabulously distinctive bottle looking like a solid block of white chocolate with a clean slice

" We would do a white Belgian chocolate cream liqueur. And we would base it on Cognac, not Irish whiskey. That way we would keep it as far away from Baileys as possible."

Brand Godet Belgian Chocolate Liqueur

USP New top tier in cream liqueurs

Client Mark Wilson, Baileys

Taste Belgian chocolate, cream and Cognac

Ideal drinker Lady Godiva

Launch Small-scale test

Designer Howard Waller

shaved off it. It was outrageous and everyone loved it. The name Godet had great appeal too. Any brand name with 'God' providing the first three letters was bound to be a hit. And if Godiva Belgian chocolates had ideas in this area (which they eventually did), our Olympus would be higher than theirs.

But Godet too suffered at the expense of the innovation overload at IDV. The company was growing fast, there were mergers and takeovers in the wings and this was a brand too far. We were to take some of the lessons from Godet and apply them to a brand of our own after my contract with Diageo ended. But that is another story, told in the next chapter.

In hindsight, these absurd briefs like Sheridan's or Godet could often give rise to the most elegant solutions. Sheridan's might easily have emerged as cappuccino-flavoured Baileys, same colour with a dumbed-down coffee taste. And Godet might have been Cadbury's Dairy Milk-flavoured Baileys. There was something in the apparent pointlessness of the original briefs that made us all try harder.

The mid to late 1980s, when Tim Ambler was in charge, was a period when we thought we could do anything – and quickly too. We had the team for it.

IQ
The 'think drink'

In the early nineties the Tom Peters' Brand Champions idea (see page 329) was in full swing in IDV and one of the UK directors was intrigued at the thought of competing more directly with Red Bull which was gaining real momentum in the UK. By this time, Purdey's had moved out. It was an interesting challenge. As I have said in previous chapters, the idea of going head-on against a strong competitor with a 'me-too' product is fraught with problems. (See Virgin vodka and cola, page 113.) You must have a strong competitive edge that will attract at least some of the target brand's consumers. Or instead of competing head-on, you can compete with part of the entrenched brand.

The part of Red Bull that we would aim at was Mental Energy. Red Bull was the brand for physical energy. It helped you rave all night, and kept long distance lorry drivers alert all day. (It talks about mental energy these days which suggests we may have been onto something.)

Our drink would focus on mental energy and Gordon Smith and I discovered something called 'Nootropics' (aka 'Thought Food') on the internet. These were 'smart' drugs to promote memory, attention and mental alertness. Was this a perfect solution to the brief? Red Bull could go on stimulating the body but our brand would focus on the mind. We called our brand IQ and described it as 'The Think Drink'.

I loved the bottle. We used a variation on the Purdey's shape and coloured it a vibrant metallic yellow. It had huge personality as a kind of nerdish Big Brother staring out at you from a supermarket shelf. Like a lot of our ideas it was a 'flier' but I thought it well worth trying. I was bitterly disappointed that it never got off the drawing board.

Red Bull could go on
stimulating the body but
our brand would focus
on the mind."

Brand IQ 'The Think Drink'

USP Nootropic stimulates mental energy

Client Annabel Allott, Diageo

Taste Never formulated

Ideal drinker Chess Grand Masters

Launch Never

Designer Gordon Smith

The idea of a coffee liqueur from Kenya was a natural, more so than Kenya Cane. Even back in the early seventies, Kenya coffee enjoyed a worldwide reputation for quality.

Kenya Gold
Alas, no glitter

The brief stopover in Nairobi back in 1969 that gave rise to Kenya Cane (see page 190) also spawned another idea. Coffee was one of the few consumer products associated with Kenya, famous for its high mountain Arabica coffee bean. Brands like Kahlua, from Mexico and Tia Maria from Jamaica were major coffee liqueur brands so why not a coffee liqueur from Kenya?

Mac Macpherson and his team produced a gorgeous liquid and Gerry Barney's pack design is as stylish now as it was 40 years ago. We called the brand Kenya Gold but aside from some testing in a few outlets in the UK, it never really left the ground.

I had always thought it had potential and on a trip to Chicago in the mid-1980s, I carried out a couple of focus groups amongst African-American respondents. I thought that there might be some feeling of affiliation with an African drink. But not a bit of it. These people were utterly scathing about buying an African product and thought it "risky", "potentially dangerous to health" and "totally without prestige". I was flabbergasted and saddened too. My chance of providing a helping hand to an African country sank like a stone.

Pandit's
Another passage to India

In 1990 during the period when any member of IDV's senior management could 'champion' a new idea (see 'Breakfast of champions', page 331) one of the UK company's board directors showed us a report that stated that consumption of restaurant Indian food in the UK had reached £2 billion. So why not an alcoholic beverage brand aimed at these outlets?

The result was Pandit's, a range of three items: a clear, refreshing Mango sorbet, a Kulfi (Indian ice cream) liqueur using the Baileys cream technology and a Paan drink derived from the traditional Indian mix of betel and areca nuts which was taken as a stimulant or to cleanse the palate.

The packaging was one of Gordon Smith's earliest efforts working for IDV and I thought one of the most exciting designs I had ever seen. The peacock feather motif in the bottle design was stunning as were the intricate graphics on the label. I can remember testing it in my local restaurant and after a slow start it began to establish a following. But like several other ideas, it ran into a period when IDV were engaged in merger talks with GuinnessUD and fringe ideas like that were quickly taken off the table.

Interestingly, there was 'a market in the gap' which was exploited soon after with huge success by Karan (now Lord) Bilimoria with his Cobra beer brand.

Indian food (often Bangladeshi) was huge in the UK, as it is now. Mango, Paan and Kulfi were shots in the dark and perhaps Lord Bilimoria's Cobra was an idea with greater potential.

> **"**
> You make what is to all intents a beer – and then you distil it. That was the answer. We wouldn't do a Guinness Whiskey at all. We would simply take Guinness and distil it."

Brand Distilled Guinness

Product Guinness distilled to 40% ABV

USP The world's first distilled beer

Client Brian Crean, Guinness

Taste Bourbon style with a hint of chocolate malt

Ideal drinker Jack Daniel's fans

Designer Gordon Smith

Distilled Guinness
Possibly my favourite idea ever

There are times in a career when you have an idea, inspect it, and marvel at its pure simplicity. Here was such an occasion. Everything came together in a few seconds and the solution appeared to be perfect. Unfortunately, I was the only person who felt that way. So this new drink never materialised.

Just after the merger between IDV and GuinnessUD in 1997, the new company's technical teams met in a 'hands across the sea' development project. Their brief was to consider the creation of a Guinness whiskey. They had spent some time working on this but nothing concrete had yet materialised. I was invited by Steve Wilson (Mac's successor as head of brand development), to "get involved – but be polite".

I attended a meeting, quite a large gathering, a couple of weeks later and sat listening attentively to the debate. After an hour someone turned to me and said "You've been unusually quiet. What's your take on all this?" My reply? "The difficulty, as I see it, is that to be true to the Guinness 'DNA' you would need to do an Irish whiskey. And you don't control supplies of the stuff which is mostly owned by your competitor, Pernod Ricard. And, if you did buy whiskey from them, you would be using the powerful Guinness name to take business from your Scotch whisky. Whichever way you turn, you lose out."

And then it happened. All those tedious trips around distilleries paid off once again. Something had stuck in my head and I used it here.

If you know anything about whisky distillation you will realise that the first stage in the process is fermentation. You actually make a beer – and then you distil it. That was the answer. We wouldn't do a Guinness whiskey at all. We would simply take Guinness and distil it.

There were countless advantages to this. Whisky has to be matured for three years in cask before it can be sold. Companies have a lot of money tied up in maturing stocks. Distilled Guinness could be made today and sold tomorrow. And another thing, Scotch and Irish whiskey were controlled by their associations so a number of rules had to be observed. For example, whisk(e)y has to be made in Scotland or Ireland. With Distilled Guinness we could make our own rules. It could be produced in any country where Guinness was brewed and where there was access to a distillery. Or anywhere else for that matter.

I suppose that the idea was a culmination of all the years I had spent in the drinks business. It tapped into both the technical and business knowledge that I had acquired over the previous 30 years. The beauty of it all was that it was so instant. Everything fell into place in seconds. It was a bit like the double-bottle Sheridans idea. It just happened and after that it seemed to develop a force of its own.

I was so excited I jumped into my car and drove to Gordon Smith's studio in Covent Garden. I wanted to see what Distilled Guinness would look like. We sat down at his Apple Mac and designed the bottle. To make the point that it was a Guinness product we went for a black bottle, but when we inspected it we thought it might be mistaken for a beer. To overcome that we went for an enormous 40%, so that potential buyers could be made aware that it was seriously strong.

Our last challenge was the product designation. What should we call it? The simplest route seemed like the best and we went for Distilled Guinness. After all, that's what it was. All this took was a couple of hours, which shows how quickly you could work if you knew exactly what you were trying to do. I loved the design.

We set up a couple of focus groups for the following week and faked a product using Jack Daniel's, J&B and some flavours – and we coloured it dark, like Guinness itself. I used the magazine article idea to introduce it and simply told people what it was. There was real interest and intrigue among the men we talked to, Guinness stout drinkers. There was certainly enough in distilled Guiness to encourage us to take the idea further.

Over the following months I really tried to get the company to take it on. Put some resource behind the development of the product and try it in six pubs in Stoke-on-Trent, or anywhere. Just try it out there in the market place. That's how it used to be. But it vanished into the maw of what was becoming an enormous corporation and was never seen again. Well not in my time.

I remain convinced that the idea of distilled beer is a very exciting proposition. Maybe one of the other big brewers will have a look at it.

Kai-zen
Functional food

This was an interesting departure from drinks. At the time of the Callitheke development discussed in Chapter 5 (Dexters, Aqua Libra, Purdey's and Pfaffs), the Grandmet empire (IDV's parent company) was growing and now included the US food giant Pillsbury, one of the major flour producers in the US situated in Minneapolis. At the height of Aqua Libra's success (and fame) Tim Ambler decided to see whether we could develop a new-age food idea along similar lines to the work we were doing in the non-alcoholic drinks area. This might fit into the Pillsbury portfolio of brands.

Annabel Allott, who had previously worked with me, had recently been on maternity leave and telephoned me asking if there was any work going. She couldn't have picked a better time, as we were looking for someone to do a trawl into new food trends to provide the basis for this new venture. She was an excellent analyst and came back to us with her recommendations within about eight weeks.

One of the more interesting ideas she had unearthed was a new (at that time) bestseller in the US called *Managing Your Mind and Mood Through Food* by Dr Judith J Wurtman from MIT (Massachusetts Institute of Technology). It had made it onto the US bestseller list

Food for your mood

by JANE ASPINALL/JOHN SMILEY

The signs are clear that there will be a boom in healthy eating in the 1990s. What was a trend in the last decade is fast becoming a way of life. And healthy eating is more than just calorie-counting. In this decade the shift will be towards *positive nutrition*.

Did you know, for example, that by manipulating the foods that you eat you can feel lively and mentally energised, thoroughly relaxed and wound down or even clear-headed and focussed? And you don't need pills or panaceas. You can do it with good-tasting, freshly –prepared foods.

In short, what you eat can influence how you *feel*. Foods which are high in protein but modest in fat and carbohydrate supply *tyrosine* to the brain. This tyrosine produces neuro-transmitters in the brain which speed up your response rate and enhance your state of mental alertness.

Foods which are high in Fast- release carbohydrate but low in protein and fat have the opposite effect. Carboydrate enables the brain to produce *serotonin* and that makes you feel mentally relaxed.

And food which are high in Slow-release carbohydrate make you feel unstressed and focused. They too produce serotonin in the brain but it is released slowly so you can feel clear-headed and reaxed at the same time.

The theory has been put in to practice by a team of French and Japanese neutritional scientists, and the foods they have created are called Kai-Zen. A selection of their products will be available here int he autumn.

They come in three categories: Protein, Slow-release Carbohydrate and Fast-release Carbohydrate.

There are two Kai-Zen protein boxes, a breakfast box and a lunch box. Each contains an interesting and imaginative selection of foods which will provide the necessary mental stimulus required. The Kai-Zen Slow-release Carbohydrate boxes are also for breakfast and lunch. They are high in fibre and all foods are made only form unrefined carbohydrate. Their function is to help you feel clear-headed and focused.

The Kai-Zen Fast-release Carbohydrate pack contains products similar in appearance to freshly-cooked wholemeal cakes. They too are high in fibre and are designed to help you relax and wind down.

Kai-Zen will also be introducing a range of compatible drinks, each desighed to accompany the various food boxes. A soft drink which is high in carbohydrate for example would nullify the effect of a protein meal.

They also suggest a three to four hour time gap between switching from, say, protein to carbohydrate foods to ensure that the effect is maximised.

Kai-Zen foods will be sold in traditional Japanese bento boxes and the samples of foods we tried were exquisitely presented. They looked appetising and tasted delicious. They are all ready-to-eat and made with freshly prepared ingredients.

Initially, Kai-Zen products will only be available via direct delivery to offices in the City and West End. In the longer term they aim to sell through high quality food shops – in the chill cabinet- and a Kai-Zen shop is also being planned.

We found the whole idea intriguingly different but it remains to be seen what the British consumer will think. Would it be a passing fad or something that could become a regular purchase item

A complicated stimulus to feed into a focus group and yet I was surprised at the widespread enthusiasm for the idea.

and seemed to offer up exactly the kind of 'soft' health proposition we were after.

The central idea in the book was that if you could manage the type of food that you ate at certain times you could affect your mood and mental performance. If you ate protein on its own, it would stimulate mental energy. So if you were making a presentation or a public appearance that was the food for you. Complex carbohydrates, on the other hand, could help with focus and concentration – for example, if you were preparing a paper or writing a book. And the final item in the trinity was simple carbohydrate which could provide a quick-fix energy boost.

Dr Wurtman's wasn't the only book on the subject and the whole notion of 'food combining' was also emerging as a growing health trend. Or was it a fad? Being a non-scientist, I was quick to become enthusiastic about this, but more serious protagonists like Mac Macpherson were less starry-eyed. I can remember Mac saying to me that "Mood food was about as scientific as horoscopes!"

But Tim's enthusiasm and whip-cracking was infectious and we powered ahead anyway. And he liked Annabel's style so much that he later invited her into the company to manage the development.

Like Callitheke, it was great fun doing it but in this case even Tim did not have the power to talk Pillsbury into taking it to market. We had the vision of opening two small kiosk-style outlets in the City of London where we would make our 'mood food' available to bankers and traders who might need the kinds of energy enhancement we were offering.

We saw the two small kiosk idea as being based on the beginnings of the McDonald's operation in San Bernardino, California back in 1937. Modern day UK chains like Pret A Manger started that way and it seemed like the perfect low-cost model for us.

We named the range Kai-zen, using the Japanese term for continuous improvement. It sounded interesting and very contemporary at the time. It sounds pretty good now too. Annabel and a designer called Darrell Ireland did a terrific job of creating the virtual outlets for it and we even commissioned a range of food and drink products. The advertisement gives a good idea of what the 'brand' looked like and was designed to help us make a convincing sale of the idea to Pillsbury and the high-ups in Grandmet.

Annabel and her team did a terrific job, creating delicious recipes, beautiful packaging and even going so far as to produce architectural designs for the kiosks themselves.

We did some focus groups, presenting the idea to educated, health-conscious men and women. We were really encouraged by their enthusiasm for the idea. Its underlying hypotheses had become topical in the more avant-garde magazines at the time. As you will see if you read the editorial, it was a detailed and complicated idea and yet most people really warmed to its thesis and gave us a great deal of encouragement to take it further. (Notice the 'positive nutrition' idea we had created for Callitheke. It would be food that was 'better for you' rather than 'less bad'.)

The idea was presented as an extract from a made-up magazine called *The Food Review* and it was a pretty complicated story. Our research respondents really got into minutiae and showed considerable interest in trying out the products. Looking through contemporary magazines at the time, I noticed that some of the articles were quite detailed and technical, so I guess I should not have been surprised.

Sadly, we failed to sell Kai-Zen to Pillsbury who were perhaps more interested in frozen products that could be sold nationally in the US market. This type of 'blue skies' thinking was not on its agenda at the time. But again, it was a very exciting development with which to be associated. Perhaps some enlightened modern developer like Pret A Manger might be interested in a venture of this kind.

"I find that when I eat the right food, I actually *feel* better. And it's especially important that I eat well during a tough working day."

Thinking person's fast food.

Kai-zen is a revolutionary new range of food products. What makes them different is that they are divided into foods which are predominantly protein *(Red Seal* foods), or slow-release carbohydrate *(Green Seal* foods).

If, as many people do, you choose to enjoy protein and carbohydrate foods on separate occasions, Kai-zen enables you to do this.

The food shown is a typical example of one of our protein recipes. Freshly-prepared and ready to eat, it is, we believe, an enjoyable way to help you through a hard working day.

KAI-ZEN Eat well, and feel good.

"My diet suggests that to feel at my best, I should eat protein and carbohydrate foods at separate times. Kai-zen really helps me to do this."

Working people often neglect their diet during a busy week. Too many cups of tea or coffee, too many soft drinks, and not enough good, healthy food.

The Kai-zen range of foods and drinks is especially suited to people who work long hours and don't have time to watch what they're eating.

Kai-zen is not a punishing regime. It is a delicious-tasting range of foods and drinks, ideal for people who are working in the 'fast lane'.

There are two categories of Kai-zen foods. *Red Seal* foods are predominantly protein, and *Green Seal* foods are carbohydrate.

Some people believe that protein foods will release mental energy, and that complex carbohydrate foods will help with focus and concentration. Kai-zen makes no claims, but believes that people should have the opportunity to try these ideas out for themselves.

KAI-ZEN Eat well, and feel good.

Tuesday lunch time and Thursday lunch time.

We did these ads to bring Kai-Zen to life. They never ran.

Fridge Fresh
The egg and I

The early seventies, when Hugh and I went out on our own, was a tough period in the UK. 1974 was the year of the 'three-day week' in British manufacturing. To keep our small business going, we resorted to developing speculative ideas which we would take to companies in the hope that they would employ us to help bring them to market.

On a trip to New York I was watching breakfast television and noticed a commercial for Arm & Hammer Baking Soda. It said that if you put an open box of baking soda into your refrigerator, it would magically prevent the migration of odours. Your milk and butter would no longer taste of fish or pickles.

Back in the UK, I passed the idea on to Bob Wagner and Kevin Twedell, designers who were occupying a room in our offices in London's Soho. It was an idle question rather than a brief so I wasn't really expecting anything.

A few days later they emerged with an intriguing illustration of a blue plastic egg with holes at either end. It was designed to fit into the refrigerator's egg tray. We completed the branding by calling it Fridge Fresh and I consulted Mac Macpherson at IDV to discuss the technology. He was one of the few chemists I knew.

"Baking soda is fine" he said "but activated charcoal is very much better. It's all about surface area. Eight grams of charcoal will have about the same area as two football fields. That will provide a massive surface area on which the odours can be absorbed". Activated charcoal had been used in gas masks during the wars, so if it was good enough to beat mustard gas it would surely combat pickled herring.

We put the idea onto paper and set off to try and sell it to interested companies across the UK. There was a lot of superficial interest. The egg was an arresting gimmick and since almost all households owned a refrigerator, the potential market could be huge. The trouble was we couldn't provide physical evidence that it worked so we couldn't clinch a sale.

The idea lay dormant on my desk for months till a friend from a previous life, Ray Davis, visited us for lunch. He fell in love with the idea and offered to help us manufacture the product and take it to market. We balked at first. We knew nothing about manufacturing and selling. But Ray was very persuasive.

Fridge Fresh was moderately successful. Ray had enormous energy and drive and after a kick-start in Boots the Chemist in the UK, he managed to sell it in a number of countries abroad. It was small stuff in the overall scheme of things but generated some much needed cash for all of us. And we even created two more eggs, one containing silica gel called Cracker Crisp to keep biscuits fresh and another with a sachet of anthracite (coal) to enliven salad vegetables.

When Hugh and I parted company in 1983, we sold our shares to Ray. He later sold the brand on to a company called Dylon and, as far as I know, Fridge Fresh still exists.

We used the line 'No more kipper-flavoured milk' to advertise Fridge Fresh on bus sides, the only medium we could afford. I fondly recall a traffic jam near my house where four buses in line paraded our campaign for all to see.

Chapter Nine
Coole Swan:
finally, a drink
of our own

I left Diageo in 2005 after 36 years. The company had become by far the largest drinks company in the world, but the people and approaches had changed. I was 67-years old and keen to stay in the game. I was to embark on an adventure which would take me far out of my comfort zone. But it was an amazing experience.

When I think back, I was isolated from most of the tough stuff that attaches to working for a company. All I had to do was to come up with ideas. Other people looked at production, finance and marketing.

Now that I was working on a brand of my own, I came to realise how difficult things could be here at the deep end.

I met up with my senior IDV client Tim Ambler in late 2005, just before I left Diageo. Tim had been out of IDV since 1991, having become a celebrated professor of marketing at London Business School. He mentioned that he'd been in Dublin and had met up with David Phelan, my client from Baileys 'The Whiskey' days (see Chapter 6). David wanted me to get in touch.

Over the previous five years, David and Pat Rigney, my client for the coffee cream liqueur Sheridan's (see Chapter 8), had gone out on their own and developed a successful Irish vodka brand called Boru, named for Brian Boru, the last king of Ireland. They had done it for themselves, not for a big company. Grey Goose had made the point that vodka didn't have to come from Russia, Poland or Sweden (see Chapter 7). If France was a credible product source, why not Ireland?

Pat and David's Boru
Vodka from Ireland

I eventually got in touch with David and he said that he and Pat had sold their shares in Boru to a US company and he was looking for a new start-up and wondered whether I would be interested. Did I fancy becoming involved in owning a brand instead of creating it for somebody else?

There was no immediate work in prospect for me after Diageo and I felt that I was too young to concentrate on golf or gardening. Yes, I was up for it. David had blazed a trail in terms of setting up a company and financing it, so he would look after the business and sales side. But we would need another partner, someone who could handle the technical aspects of whatever we decided to do.

Adrian Walker, the third member of the old Baileys whiskey team and a long-time colleague (Cîroc, Tanqueray Ten and Smirnoff Black), had also left Diageo and was working for a product development consultancy. I got in touch, Adrian expressed interest and the three of us agreed to meet in Dublin a few weeks later in November 2005. We would see if we could come up with anything interesting.

Looking for an opportunity
Stores were better than scores

We met in a private room at David's golf club outside Dublin. We gave ourselves a day and a night to come up with something. Much of the time was spent talking about old times and old colleagues. We used casual gossip to avoid facing up to the issues. It sometimes happens like that.

After ploughing through columns of figures and discussing what other people were doing we were nowhere. So we took ourselves off to a large liquor store on the outskirts of Dublin and roamed around chatting and looking. And then we saw it, plain as day. We were looking at the space occupied by cream liqueurs and there was Baileys with the lion's share, surrounded by copy-cat brands like Carolans, Emmets and Amarula.

The interesting thing was that the competitors were all cheaper than Baileys. Unlike vodka, whiskey or gin, there were no premium products on the cream shelf. Baileys was the crème de la crème, and the competition was bargain basement.

Crème de la crème
Back to Baileys basics

So there we had it. We would introduce the world's first premium cream liqueur. Premiums were cropping up all over the place. They were becoming significant in vodka and gin. And they had always been significant in whisky. They were now springing up in all kinds of categories. In the drinks business we had done it ourselves with Cîroc and Tanqueray Ten and in other fields, like food and confectionery, Green & Black's, Häagen-Dazs, Innocent and Yakult were all playing to the new music of 'buy less but buy better'.

Eighty million bottles of cream liqueur were sold world-wide every year. Why were they all at Baileys' price or below? We had looked at the possibility of a premium cream with a chocolate cream liqueur brand called Godet years ago (see Chapter 8) but the company never gave it a real chance. We worked out that if we, the Three Musketeers, could achieve a level of only 1 per cent of Baileys' volume in five years, we would have a very profitable business.

Adrian parted company with his consultancy, David was extricating himself from his Boru commitments and we started our business in July 2006. We had set our sights on a launch in Dublin in March 2007 in order to get the business set up to trade in the UK and US for the key pre-Christmas season later that year. It was 'game on'.

If you don't have any money...
...the stuff in the bottle has to taste amazing

One of the comforting thoughts early on was that cream liqueurs were a 'taste' category. In the same way that Green & Black's was able to develop and offer the consumer a perceptibly better-tasting chocolate bar, we should technically be able to achieve this with a cream liqueur.

Creams were easier than mainline spirits like vodka where differences between products were minuscule. We could engineer a real difference. A plan was emerging with Green & Black's providing an excellent model. It was based on judgment rather than lots of research. We didn't have the money for that. We wanted to look different from Baileys and all other cream liqueurs. And our product had to taste better.

If you look back at the Baileys chapters (see Chapters 1 and 2), there was no burning technical issue that said the product must be chocolate-brown. It just came out that way when we used Cadbury's Drinking Chocolate in our prototype. That is what we presented to the Irish and that is what they liked. They went on to use caramel in Baileys to match that colouring.

Ours would be an entirely natural product. It would be a gorgeous, appetising creamy-white like the Godet product. No caramel, no colourants, no additives. Our cream would come from rain-sodden county Cavan, the finest cream in Ireland.

Existing cream liqueurs were too sweet and unsophisticated. We did a lot of tasting of Baileys and other cream liqueurs from around the world and our overwhelming conclusion was that they were sweet, far too sweet. Their flavour seemed to be 'dumbed down' so that they would appeal to a wider, less discriminating audience. We wanted our product to be 30 per cent less sweet than other brands in the same way that Green & Black's was less sweet than Cadbury's Dairy Milk.

We accepted that we couldn't be all things to all people. We would court a smaller, more discerning following. If we weren't better, genuinely better, we were dead. For a tiny embryo company like ours to survive in the predatory marketplace 'out there' we had to deliver a superb product. And unlike other cream liqueurs, we would be proud of our ingredients and proclaim them on our bottle.

Adrian determined the ingredients we would need and we agreed that we should source the best varieties that we could get. We went for vanilla from Madagascar, cocoa from Côte d'Ivoire and Belgian white chocolate. These were the best components we could find.

Our most important decision centred on choosing the whiskey. We tasted them all. In his search for the perfect product, Adrian underwent the pleasantly onerous task of sampling every single whiskey available in Ireland. He was looking for a soft, smooth whiskey that would blend seamlessly with our vanilla, cocoa, chocolate and cream. He eventually found it, a beautiful Irish single malt, but confidentiality doesn't allow me to reveal its name. He put all these together, tweaked a little here and there and 231 iterations later we had our product.

As I hope I have emphasised throughout this book, we have always been fanatical about the stuff that goes into the bottle. And our zeal reached new heights with this brand of our own. The product was exactly what we were after.

Building our brand
Ditching the cream conventions

Our next issue was the brand, including the name and the pack design. We had more or less left Adrian to it with the product and no one could have been more assiduous than he in achieving perfection. He left a trail of sample bottles at David's house in Dublin, at my house in London and at the creamery in Cavan. Name and pack design would be something else. We expected hot debate.

Our first decision on branding was that we would be as different from the conventional run of cream liqueurs as we could possibly be. The Bob Wagner-designed Baileys theme of short, squat brown bottles regaled with an Irish pastoral cartouche had become the world-wide convention for cream liqueurs. We had broken the pattern ourselves with Sheridan's and Godet, but the rest of them were still playing the same tune.

We would create a convention of our own. I would put together a glossary of terms that would guide the design brief which we would give to designer friend Gordon Smith.

As with many other projects, agreeing on a name was one of the most vexed areas. And when you are naming a brand that is co-owned by three opinionated guys, it was a formula for conflict. There were occasions where we nearly came to blows.

Since this was my field, the responsibility for coming up with the name was mine. It took up more time than anything else I did on this development and there were many agonising moments. The process of creating for oneself seemed so much harder than doing it for someone else. I wanted something totally different, unlike any other cream liqueur in the world.

The first inspiration came on a drive from Cavan to Dublin airport where we saw the most spectacular rainbow. It seemed to fill the sky and the colours were bright and vibrant. I have no religion in me but I couldn't help thinking that it was a sign from somewhere. So Rainbow became my recommendation and I was prepared to fight for it. For Adrian it was loathing at first sight. He hated it. But he's a very polite hater. David was more diplomatic and said it was a 'powerful' name and very 'elemental'. He just wanted me to get on with it so we could brief the pack design and get ready for market.

I dug my heels in and became unreasonably dogmatic about the name, so we briefed Gordon to use it on his bottle design. We even put it into focus groups in London and Dublin. There were a few negative comments but not enough to force a change. The illustration on page 321 shows how our brand was first presented to prospective buyers.

William Butler Yeats trying
to think of a name for a new
Irish Cream liqueur.

Then, to everyone else's delight, we discovered that the name wasn't available. Rainbow was owned by a company in the US. We could not use it. I was secretly relieved. The name Rainbow hadn't exactly passed with flying colours.

Hurrah for W B Yeats
A whiter shade of Coole

We were getting used to the last plane out of Dublin and looking for inspiration one evening I picked up a paperback book of Yeats' poetry. Past experience has shown that this kind of approach never ever works, but you live in hope. Brand naming isn't always a logical deliberate act. It is often the outcome of a happy accident.

In this case it did work, but not in the way I expected. I discovered one of Yeats' most famous poems, a wistful reflection on the passing of time called *The Wild Swans at Coole*. It was written at Coole Park, the elegant stately home of Lady Isabella Gregory who was one of his benefactors.

There has been a tradition of naming drinks after birds – Famous Grouse, Wild Turkey Bourbon and, of course, Grey Goose. There is even a South African brandy rather cumbersomely named Flight of the Fish Eagle. I thought that Wild Swan would fit in very well and it had a nice intellectual Irish connection. As we were after more discerning drinkers, that wouldn't hurt.

David and Adrian went to New York to sound out potential distributors over there and while the response to packaging and product was highly favourable, there were some rumbling concerns about the name. They felt that Wild Swan was sailing too close to Wild Turkey's wind and that we might attract some litigation which we could ill afford.

I was away in Australia at the time, watching cricket in Brisbane, when I received a call from Adrian. "We are changing it to Coole Swan" he said. "It's safer and we also think it's better." I gulped but had no grounds for debate. I was at the other end of the world enjoying myself while they were both slaving away at the coal face.

My objection was probably based on the fact that the name Coole Swan was Not-Invented-Here – by me, I mean. In the world of ideas, hubris can reign for anyone. But in hindsight, they were right. I now really love the name. It sums up the product and Coole Swan provides ownership of the word 'cool', which is no bad thing in the youth-orientated world we live in.

Utterly Coole by Gordon Smith
Designed to perfection

The last link in the chain was the Coole Swan bottle, engineered by Adrian Walker and designed by Gordon Smith with a little help from me in devising the brief and writing the words.

We set out to create a new vocabulary for cream liqueur design. Our words were 'cold', 'clean', 'fresh', 'creamy', 'subtle' and 'complex'. We would concentrate on 'cold' colours like blue, green, black and silver. No warm reds, browns or gold. 'Fresh' was my key word. At the back of my mind, Absolut was the model. We would be selling cool, fresh Irish cream.

This is what Gordon delivered. It was magnificent, beyond our wildest expectations.

The first thing to strike me about the bottle was that it was frosted white flint, not dark glass like other cream liqueurs. This was Adrian's doing. He discovered that white glass, as long as it was frosted, would provide protection for the product against ultra-violet light. It would be expensive but it looked stunning. And Adrian had also found the inspiration for the bottle shape. It was based on the design for a 19th

"

We set out to create
a new vocabulary for
cream liqueur design.
Our words were 'cold',
'clean', 'fresh', 'creamy',
'subtle' and 'complex'. We
would concentrate on cold
colours like blue, green,
black and silver."

Brand Coole Swan Superior Cream Liqueur

USP Super-premium cream

Clients David Phelan, Adrian Walker and me

Taste Chocolate, whiskey and cream

Ideal drinker Wife of Diageo's CEO

Launch 2007

Designer Gordon Smith

century milk bottle which he'd found in a friend's collection.

It was Howard Waller who taught me that "God, not the devil, is in the details" and we certainly looked closely at every tiny aspect of this design. On the front, we took two utterly mundane elements and made them work overtime for us. Instead of the traditional 'Serve cold' we transformed our legend to 'Beautiful chilled'. I had adapted that from old-fashioned Indian Kingfisher beer labels which I remembered read 'Most thrilling chilled'.

Then I appropriated a line from my Stubbs Australian White rum design (see Chapter 7) and put 'Made only in Ireland' on the front label. This was a selling statement about the brand, adding a little emotive 'oomph' to otherwise workaday 'Produce of Ireland' which you would normally find.

On the back we did something no other cream liqueur had done before. We wrote a detailed description of all our ingredients. We wanted to show our pride in the product and its utterly mouthwatering recipe. Anyone know what goes into Baileys?

Coole Swan was spectacularly launched at the Irish National Gallery on 19th March 2007 and it is now making its way in the world. The three of us have moved on to new ventures though we all retain shares in the brand. Its progress through the wide world of drink will no doubt

The cherry on the top

There was a nice quirk at the end of this process. There on the base at the back of Gordon's bottle mould was a blind-embossed motif which was puzzling. We asked Gordon what it was. "It's a sort of tattoo" he said. "I put it on for a bit of fun. It's a cat lapping up a bowl of cream like in the famous old Baileys commercial. Of course you'll never do it." Well, it was our brand and we thought the idea was brilliant. So there it stayed.

be the subject of another story.

The brand was everything we hoped that it would be and received major accolades around the world. In 2008, it received a 5* highest recommendation from Paul Pacult, in his *Spirit Journal*, a fine tribute from one of the industry's true pundits. Coole Swan also received a 96-100 rating in *Wine Enthusiast's Buyer's Guide* in 2009. And its finest achievement was its award as the 'World's Best Liqueur' and Double Gold Medal winner at the San Francisco World Spirits competition.

'Skin in the Game'
The bit that can really bite you

Having mainly been involved in the origination of ideas for other people, creating a brand of my own provided some rude awakenings. If you think back to Smirnoff Black which I wrote about in Chapter 7, I was the person who recommended that we make the vodka in a pot still – in Moscow. But I didn't have to source the still, ship it to Cristall distillery and teach the Russians how to use it. My adventure was all on a piece of paper and from the comfort of my own office. Having 'skin in the game', as the commercial people tell it, was an entirely different affair.

First, there was the assault on our own bank accounts or, in my case, my pension pot. We paid for the flash launch party in Dublin. And there was a constant drag on our personal finances as the world moved into economic meltdown and it became harder and harder to find outside funding.

Coole Swan was also physically demanding. Aside from the dawn flights to Ireland and the midnight returns, we also did a lot of personal selling. I can remember Adrian selling 95 bottles on one St Valentine's Day at The Whisky Exchange near London Bridge; and my partner, Barbara Bryant, would traipse to John Lewis at Bluewater in Kent,

Wild swans, not necessarily at Coole, which inspired our brand name.

to Harrods, and to Selfridges stores in London, Birmingham and Manchester for exhausting days' tasting and selling.

I can even recall a snowy day pre-Christmas when I had a tasting to do at a store in Maida Vale. My leg was in plaster after a foot operation and most transport was at a standstill because of the weather. But I managed the two-mile hobble plus another four hours at the 'hustings' selling our beloved brand.

This was my first real experience of direct selling at the tender age of 69. But it was gratifying to realise that Coole Swan was quite an easy sale. Of course I knew the spiel – I'd written it – so that part was easy. After that your instinct took over.

Most people were knocked out by the appearance of the pack. It was cool and elegant and nothing like traditional 'Wagnerian'

Coole Swan gets to the top of the charts

Shortly after launch, Coole Swan achieved a 5 Star rating from *Bev.X* in the US and was voted amongst the top ten spirits of 2009.

"We have never seen a finer cream liqueur. It has the pleasing and somewhat nostalgic appearance of a vanilla malt with its creamy off-white tones. The nose is a subtle and complex interplay of dark chocolate, vanilla cream and marzipan. The palate is silky smooth and rich with subtle fruit notes. Elegant and wonderfully styled. As a topper, this unique liqueur is offered in a fresh, sleek and modern package."

Coole Swan was awarded Double Gold as the best liqueur in the San Francisco World Spirits Competition and received a 5 Star rating in Paul Pacult's influential *Spirit Journal*. This was praise indeed for our small enterprise. We could do it for ourselves too.

cream liqueurs. And the cold white liquid looked extremely inviting, compelling most people to want to taste it.

There were occasional refusers, both men and women, but they were easily persuaded to think again. Coole Swan had something for everyone.

Coole Swan made a great first impression via its bottle, so much more elegant and sophisticated than dumpy Baileys and its look-alikes. When Belgian white chocolate and Irish single malt whiskey were mentioned, enthusiasm began to show. After that, when people tasted the cool, luscious product, conversion was immediate. This face-to-face selling was a lot easier than I had expected. But then, I knew we had a fabulous product.

In the drinks business advocacy is all important. The aim is to spread the word. I cannot begin to count the number of people I have sat alongside on aeroplanes, at sports events or at dinner parties when I have chatted them up and tried to sell them Cîroc, The Singleton, Tanqueray Ten, Coole Swan and many others. And it was never a forced sell. I genuinely believed, and still do, that the products were excellent, the best they could be. I couldn't imagine myself having the same amount of enthusiasm for detergents or dog food. Booze is a much more sociable category.

Epilogue
Origins of an iconoclast

I was born and raised in 'the colonies'. My mother wanted me to be a lawyer but my university grades had other ideas. My father suggested I go into advertising. I'd never heard of it but I agreed. Then I became a new product creator through luck as much as anything else. And what luck it was.

It is likely that I inherited my enthusiasm for alcohol from my father who always enjoyed a tipple, usually gin at lunch time and whisky in the evening. In South Africa, in pursuit of bargain prices, we seemed to get obscure Scotch brands that I was later to discover were rarely visible in the rest of the world. Asking for Red Hackle or Crawford's wouldn't have struck any chords in London or New York. Aside from the likes of Sweet Rosinke, a puckeringly sweet kosher-for-Passover concoction which was always around, we rarely had wine at home. The only one I can remember with any clarity was a Portuguese Vinho Verde called Casal Garcia which my parents would share on their wedding anniversary. This knowledge hardly equipped me for confronting IDV's Masters of Wine in my future incarnation.

'Button-down' beginnings
'A manicure to fit your pocket'

My moderate commercial skills were definitely inherited from my father who tried many things but none of them successfully. On his advice, I went into advertising. But, as the old saying goes, 'Don't tell my mother. She thinks I play the piano in a brothel'. For two years after leaving university I worked for a Johannesburg ad agency called Afamal. (Today it sounds like some over-the-counter stomach medicine.) I was put onto a training programme and my mentor, an expat Englishman called D Owen Barrett, decided to turn me into an account executive, a kind of middleman between the agency's creative people and our clients.

But the department I most enjoyed was copywriting and I can recall delivering 'A Manicure to Fit Your Pocket' for a product called the Gem Patent Fingernail Clipper. The client summarily dismissed my masterpiece to replace it with 'The World's Finest Fingernail Clipper'. It is strange to reflect that my first bout of professional hubris was brought about by a product as prosaic as that.

My boss at Afamal had a 1930s view of salaries in the business. He felt that people should pay him to work in his agency. As a result, I received barely enough to live on. In desperation I resigned and took a market research job with Lever Brothers in Durban even though I had very little knowledge of what market research was. But it paid three times my advertising pittance, a princely £900 per year.

As it turned out, after about six months in the job, I concluded that research was not for me: the people were pretty lacklustre and the work was not to my taste. Finding out which detergent people had bought in the last seven days or tabulating worldwide sales figures for margarines didn't feature in Vance Packard's *The Hidden Persuaders*. I'd generated a bit of money, bought a yellow 1952 Peugeot 203 and was beginning to feel like a man of substance. But the time had come to liquidate my assets and take the biggest plunge of my life: I lashed out £37 for a one-way ticket to Southampton on the RMS Cape Town Castle.

I had it all worked out: two years in London, two in New York on Madison Avenue, then a road trip to Rio and a boat back home. I sailed from Port Elizabeth, saying goodbye to South Africa in the November of 1961, two days after my twenty-third birthday.

Go North, young man
London beckons

The boat trip was an endless party with imported Amstel and Tuborg beer costing 5p a bottle – in today's decimal currency – and twenty cigarettes for 10p. Best of all there were attractive and spirited girls in abundance. I decided on the intellectual approach, flaunting my new-found though decidedly 'agricultural' bridge-playing skills as a means of meeting them. The Charles Atlas body beautiful types took the high ground during the first few days but bridge proved pretty successful later.

The food was dire – but who ate? There were five hundred men and a thousand women and each night we danced, or staggered to the music of the Nathan Ginsberg Quartet. No. 1 in the charts at that time was the theme music from the film *Exodus*. How innocent we were then. Ginsberg was a much better musician than he was a goalkeeper. I had seen him let in 18 goals for Welkom United against Durban City a few months earlier.

There were three people I met on board who were all going to London to storm the advertising world. And they pretty well did. Barry Lategan would become a celebrated fashion photographer who helped put Twiggy, the fashion model and sixties icon, on the map; Roy Carruthers was one of the co-creators of the famous 'Happiness is a cigar called Hamlet' campaign; and Len Weinreich was to write the hilarious 'French Adore Le Piat d'Or' campaign for a brand that I was to create 15 years later. He would also write that brilliant 'cat lapping the cream' TV commercial for Baileys.

We stopped for 24 hours at Las Palmas – my first real experience of 'overseas' as we South Africans called everywhere else – and I bought a bottle of Bacardi from a suspicious outlet called Madame Jesus. I had never actually seen a bottle in the flesh before but had read all about it in Hemingway novels. It was a real thrill. In fact it was so exciting that we opened it while negotiating the Bay of Biscay. It was filled with rather brackish water. No doubt Madame Jesus had been walking on it (in unwashed feet) before consigning it to bottle. Bacardi was to become an important theme in my future working life.

Southampton at dawn in the midst of English winter was not an attractive sight. But we had arrived. On the coach trip up to London we stopped at a pub for warm beer and ungenerously filled sandwiches lubricated with Stork margarine. En route, perhaps to cheer us up, the driver showed us the tree on the A3 at the Guildford by-pass where the racing driver Mike Hawthorn crashed his Jaguar and was killed.

We alighted in Earl's Court and were billeted five to a room, sleeping on mattresses at the Overseas Visitors Club. Like all good colonial boys, we went immediately to look at Eros, the essential port of call for everyone visiting London for the first time. It was disappointingly small, and we couldn't understand why the pubs were shut at three in the afternoon.

My first two months were spent looking for a place to live, searching for a job, being diagnosed as suffering from scurvy and enduring a 24-hour bout of pneumonia. My first accommodation was near Selfridges in Oxford Street which, in hindsight, was a strange choice. It was right in the middle of shopper's London, a long way from the sociability of places like Kensington or Chelsea.

A London adman at last
Lunching for England

Job hunting was a problem as the ad agencies were in party mode throughout November and December – and they really knew how to party in those days. I was offered an interview, but it was for a posting in Kuala Lumpur. Did I really want to go back to the colonies so soon after arriving in London? What kind of expat would I make? Since it was the only show in town I thought I'd follow it up but, sadly for him and luckily for me, the man who interviewed me died during the Christmas festivities.

I was also subjected to a kind of pseudo-psychological assessment by the J Walter Thompson agency called 'Progressive Matrices'. Whatever it was these techniques were designed to tease out, I didn't have it. The test was administered by a woman called Valerie Kennedy Brown whose name could have come from *Just William*, I thought.

In desperation and with about £5 left in my bank account I decided that the 'cold call' approach was my last resort. I put on my only suit and stormed the offices of Benton & Bowles (B&B) at 197 Knightsbridge. The two gorgeous receptionists seemed to take pity on me and intimated that they thought the agency was looking for people. I asked if I could use the internal telephone, talked to the director who was hiring, and managed to organise to meet him that evening.

My interview with Bruce Rhodes went well and I was offered a job as assistant account executive on Procter & Gamble's Camay Soap account on a salary of £900 per year. I was ecstatic.

It is interesting to look at my salary then against its purchasing power at the time. Rent was about £3 per week or £150 pa; beer (mild or bitter) was 7p a pint and cigarettes in London were about 20p for a packet. You could get a plate of lamb and mushroom Madras at an Indian restaurant for 25p and a tailor-made suit from Burton's cost me £12.

These were the 'lunching days' and there was a French restaurant near our office called La Surprise that was a regular watering hole for B&B executives. Lunching was almost a religion at Benton & Bowles in the sixties and we invariably went the whole hog with aperitifs, wine and cognac to finish.

When business entertaining lost its tax-deductible status in 1964, a 'Yellow Memo' was circulated by our American managing director P Townsend Griffin. In it he firmly suggested that in the interest of economy, we should discourage the offering of 'post-prandial (his words) cordials' to our clients. To keep the agency solvent, we switched from cognac to port.

I had five very happy years at B&B and made a number of friends. There were several colleagues who were to become leading lights in the ad business a few years later. Charles Saatchi and John Hegarty started their careers there, the Bobs, Geers and Gross of 'Flour Graders' advertising fame, were there too. Roy Carruthers (a Cape Town Castle acquaintance) and Tim Warriner, the 'Hamlet' creatives, also passed through, as did Frank Lowe and Richard French, both of whom were to set up their own agencies.

It was an establishment that thought it punched above its weight but was actually quite conservative. It was a London equivalent of Stirling Cooper in the TV series Mad Men. We were owned by Americans and dominated by their clients Procter & Gamble, S C Johnson and General

Learning the ropes

One of the brands I worked on was P&G's liquid cleaner Mr Clean and P&G, known at that time as 'the deadly Headley' (they had taken over a UK company called Thomas Headley) were pretty rigid in their treatment of agencies. They had a strapline for Mr Clean which to this day is emblazoned on my frontal lobes. It was: 'Mr Clean cleans faster and easier than any other soap, detergent, powder or scourer you've ever used.' And it had to be said twice in every TV commercial. Turgid as it might have been, it made its point.

There were welcome escapes for me to Kerrygold butter, Lyons teas and Personna razor blades. The last-named was a competitor to Wilkinson Sword stainless steel blades which had just come onto the market. Wilkinson had been so successful that demand was far outstripping supply. Legend had it that they distributed their product via a tailored flunkey in a white Rolls Royce and would only offer six packets of blades per outlet. I don't know of anyone who actually witnessed this, but it sure sounded good.

Foods. In those days, for American companies, the UK was almost on a par with New Hampshire or Delaware, too small to be of consequence.

My eventual departure from B&B was triggered by an utterly irrational decision on my part. My then flatmate and fellow immigrant from South Africa, Richard French, had his salary increased to £2,000 pa while mine was only put up to £1,900. It was preposterous and an affront and I took my high dudgeon across Hyde Park to Erwin Wasey Ruthrauff & Ryan (aka E W Ratrace & Ruin) another American subsidiary in Paddington opposite the station.

But after my wonderful introduction to British business at Benton & Bowles, my trip across the park turned out to be a mistake, so I started to search for something new. I was 29 and needed to look ahead and try to plan my career.

Wall's
Sausage makers to the gentry

I was offered a job with Lintas (I couldn't help seeing it as an anagram for 'Stalin'), an advertising agency owned by Unilever. Their offices were in New Fetter Lane, half way between El Vino's, the famous Fleet Street wine bar, and Gamages, a 1930s-style department store which must have been the dowdiest shop in England. I thought it the kind of place where you'd find dandruff on the carpets. It was, as it is now, a 'neither-one-thing-nor-another' part of London.

Lintas wasn't great. The name was a typical Unilever mnemonic, Levers International Advertising Service. I worked on very boring accounts like Wall's Sausages and Gibbs Toothpaste. I remember my first trip around the Wall's factory hosted by a gentleman called Colonel Skee. He proudly proclaimed that Wall's in Willesden had "the fastest slaughter line in Europe". It wasn't a happy thought.

Wall's had airs rather than ears and they saw themselves as quite posh. They referred to the cellophane that wrapped their sausages as 'their livery'. Peter Phillips, father of Mark, worked there though we never met. Mark was Princess Anne's first husband.

On one occasion we presented a new TV campaign featuring sausages sizzling in a frying pan with a voiceover done by the popular English comedian Terry Scott. "Oh no, no, no" said one of their directors "we can't have people with that kind of accent talking about our sausages. We carry the Royal Warrant". We were talking about sausages here, also

Companies have personalities too

Unilever companies all had their own distinct personalities in those days. Wall's went for chaps from decent public schools. Graduates were untrustworthy. Wall's' strategic thinking was governed by the short-termism which came with killing today and selling tomorrow. Birds Eye was the exciting new kid on the block with the buccaneering spirit epitomised by its figurehead, Captain Birdseye. And, strangely, its first chief executive was called James Parratt.

I can remember a study done among primary school children in the 1990s where they were asked to name the most famous captains of all time. Much to adland's delight the order of recall in descending order was Birds Eye, Crunch, Kirk and finally, a long way down, Captain Cook, the man who discovered Australia.

Gibbs and the toothpaste people were quite dull though new Signal – the toothpaste with the mouthwash in the stripe – had been introduced earlier. I was told that the idea for the stripe was cooked up by an Italian dessert chef in a New York restaurant in 1955. Lever Brothers people, perhaps unexpectedly, were the cerebral intelligentsia of the corporation. Though, in hindsight, it was difficult to reconcile this sophistication with the decidedly unpalatable 'Understains' advertising for one of their failed detergent brands.

known in England as 'bangers'. Ordinary grub for good ordinary people.

I was firmly established as an account manager at Lintas and the longer I did it, the less I liked it. I thought the creative output was very so-so and was often difficult to sell to clients. And there were quite a few 'February solutions' which involved taking a bevy of model girls off to the Caribbean in the depth of English winter for a commercial shoot. That type of thing was hard to justify for sausages or toothpaste. Perhaps there was an element of envy on my part. Antigua in February had a lot going for it. I had to settle for Old Oak Lane, Willesden, not one of London's glittering areas.

Given the chance to have my time again in advertising, I would have been a copywriter. I always loved playing with words. When I started at Benton & Bowles I was forever trying to come up with lines for other people's brands.

Saved by the Bill
New business life begins

The ad business was changing. Agencies were developing new specialist service departments in package design, market research and sales promotion. Lintas was offering some of these services. Why not set up a specialist new product group, I thought? I really fancied the idea of inventing new things, getting into a creative function at last and being able to involve myself in a variety of interesting pursuits. And I would be able to do this without trampling on the creative department's toes. It was perfect.

I took the idea to our managing director, the wonderfully open-minded Bill Taylor. The agency was looking to attract outside clients and break the Unilever yoke, so why not set up a kind of 'sampler group' where outside clients could try us out on a limited basis? And if they liked us they might consider giving Lintas some of their main advertising business. The management bought the idea and in 1969, our new product group, Presight, was born. I was put together with Hugh Seymour-Davies to run the division.

Off we went selling our services, winning some and losing a few too. We created a new menthol and mint ice-blue cough sweet for Rowntree called Lyrics – to compete with Tunes – and two new children's snack foods for Birds Eye called Cheesies and Chicklets. They were bite-sized bits of cheese and chicken covered in batter. Our Chicklets bore a startling resemblance to present-day Chicken Nuggets so perhaps we

A dog's dinner

One idea that stands out was a dog food we created for the Quaker Oats company which made Chunky, famously advertised by politician and raconteur Clement Freud and his sidekick Henry the Bloodhound. We were told that 'anthropomorphism' was what dog food was all about. Get the owner enthusiastic and the dog would be a pushover.

We made up this dog's dinner in the office using instant porridge, semi-moist chunks of a meat-like substance and Bovril beef extract to add flavour. All you had to do was add boiling water, stir it around and there you had it: an aromatic beefy gourmet dinner – for dogs. I even tasted it in front of the client at the meeting to demonstrate how delicious it was.

It emerged as a brand called Hungry Hound that went into a small-scale test market. The trouble was that you had to mix it with boiling water and once it was prepared, the bouquet drove dogs crazy. They were desperate to get at it. But it had to be kept out of range to cool down for half an hour before they could eat it. It was soon withdrawn after several kitchen units had been ripped to pieces by an assembly of very hungry hounds. We concluded that perhaps we hadn't thought that one through.

can lay claim to have been the fathers of this now ubiquitous children's staple. Versions can be found at Macdonald's, Burger King, KFC and school canteens across the land.

We dealt with people on high at Unilever too and I can remember presenting to the World Yellow Fats Co-Ordinator (the Obergruppenführer of Margarine) within the forbidding bowels of Unilever House at Blackfriars. I am not sure White Fats like lard ran to a World Co-Ordinator of their own.

Despite our social differences, Hugh and I were working well together. New product development was exhilarating, terrific fun. It was a kibitzer's dream, getting involved with technical people, working with pretty home economists making prototype food products and interfering with package design and even advertising. It was what I had been made for.

Then I was sent to a Unilever seminar on market research at the hotel Regina Palace in Stresa on Lake Maggiore, Italy. It was there that I met Tom Jago and my world changed forever.

Inventing drinks for a living
Probably the best job in the world

As I hope I've communicated in these pages, mine was one of the most enjoyable jobs in the world. I visited amazing places and met wonderful people. And I loved the challenge of trying to come up with good ideas. Drink is fascinating and provides one of the many windows into people's lives.

At the time I started with IDV back in 1969 Business Class hadn't been invented so, to my surprise and delight, all long haul flights were in First. I even managed four trips on Concorde, the first about a month after its maiden flight. (Harry Hyams, my boss from my very first ad agency job in Johannesburg, was on the same flight.) And I travelled to places I never thought I would visit for work: Rio and Salvador in Brazil, Tokyo, Kyoto, Seoul, Mumbai, Nairobi, New Orleans, Los Angeles, New York, Sydney, Mauritius and even back home to South Africa. And none of the trips were 'jollys'. I can recall arriving in Seoul after 12 hours in the air and being invited to a 'trade visit'. This involved taking in half a dozen smart bars, having a whisky or two in each and then presenting myself bright-eyed for a meeting at 9am next day. That happened more than once.

The only aspect of my work that I haven't tried to teach is the business of coming up with the ideas themselves. It took about four years – from 1969 when I started to 1973 when the Baileys idea emerged – for me to develop the confidence needed to put all my eggs in a single solution basket.

I was always fascinated by techniques and procedures which helped me create new ideas. Even before I became a brand developer, I was sent on a Synectics course in London, run by one of its founders, George Prince. I'd only been with the agency for a few weeks and had no idea what Synectics was. It turned out to be a complete buzz and I went around the advertising agency where I was working offering to run sessions for all and sundry on any subject. Connie Williams, one of my clients from Heublein in the US (taken over by IDV), now heads up Synectics in the US. And Edward de Bono, the man who postulated the idea of Lateral Thinking, was one of my early heroes. Synectics, as it was then, appeared to be an operational tool to help you think laterally, so it complemented de Bono's work.

There are people who advocate sophisticated brainstorming techniques as part of comprehensive innovation packages but these never worked for me. My stimuli were a lot more down-to-earth.

Fear worked a treat. I mean the fear of failure that you might not come up with an idea that you genuinely believed in. The cold sweat induced by the imminence of a really important meeting worked wonders too. And the need to impress was a strong stimulus for creative thinking. In many cases, the more senior and powerful the client, the better the quality of the work. There is nothing like the adrenalin rush you get when you present to someone really high up in an organisation.

These people could look at the big picture. They didn't quibble or nitpick. And they wanted specific recommendations, not rafts of options. That's how things worked in their world.

But, as I hope I have shown throughout the pages of this book, you really do have to live and breathe the business. You take your problems to bed at night, sometimes you dream about them. More often than not they present themselves when you wake up in the morning. Or when you least expect them. Just keep looking. Sheridan's arrived when I saw a pint of Guinness being pulled in a Dublin airport bar at 9 in the morning ; Godet, the Belgian chocolate cream liqueur happened when I saw a Marks & Spencer Christmas ad in Baker Street station; and Red Chardonnay jumped off a very dull page about wine legislation. I would love to be able to offer a formula... but I don't think there is one.

Afterword

The method in my madness

To be good at brand development you need courageous clients. After that, you need the knowledge that comes with experience on the job. And then you need instinct. There is no magic formula. I developed a battery of simple techniques which I learned 'on the hoof'. They saved time and cut costs. They worked for me and they could work for you. And it was more simple common sense than rocket science. But I am proud of that.

→ Although this book focuses largely on my experiences in the drinks business and working for IDV/Diageo, I did venture out on numerous occasions as a brand developer. I worked for breweries including Allied, Bass, Whitbread, Watneys and Tetley Walker. And in other sectors I was employed by Rowntree Mackintosh, Quaker Oats, Unigate, Express Dairies, Wall's Meat Company, Kraft, Lever Brothers and Birds Eye. And I even worked for Bacardi after I parted company with Diageo.

And, as stated earlier, there were two homegrown ventures, Fridge Fresh in 1974 and Coole Swan in 2007.

Looking back on all my work, the same practices and principles applied across the board, give or take a few very early projects where we were feeling our way. Baileys in 1973 and Tanqueray Ten nearly 30 years later were both single solutions; Fridge Fresh and Cîroc a generation later followed similar paths.

The same approach was applied in the 1970s and in the 2000s, whether the work was for clients or for ourselves. Study the problem, present an idea, test it (modestly), change it – and then make it happen.

There were methods but they were simple ones. There might have been the odd broken paradigm along the way and even the occasional idea from 'out of the box' – but most of the ideas came from good old-fashioned linear thinking.

The real heroes of innovation in companies are the people who buy ideas. Trouble is, there aren't enough of them.

Coming up with ideas was my job. If I solved a problem, I was a hero. Or so I thought. But it wasn't true. The real heroes of innovation, especially in large corporations, were the people who *bought* outrageously different ideas. Most of the successes in this book only happened because people, often high up the ladder, made a judgment call on something that broke with prevailing tradition. Baileys would never have seen the light of day if Tom Jago had rejected it because he didn't like it; or Mac Macpherson, the chemist who had to make it, said he didn't have the knowledge; or, lastly, if the Irish end-user David Dand had taken against it. Baileys might have been strangled early, vanishing without trace.

And what might have happened if some committed manager had decided that Distilled Guinness was worth a shot? The idea was fully formed and it would have cost very little to try it out in a few bars and liquor stores. That way we could see how it fared in the real world with real people buying it and drinking it – or not. We did that for Baileys in a single pub. Only one bottle was consumed. But this tiny test gave the brand the fillip it needed to go on to greater things. Testing brands on a micro scale was the most cost-effective research we ever did.

Companies would do well to search assiduously for people who are good at buying ideas. IDV had many such individuals, mostly at the top of the organisation. Perhaps HR people could turn their attention to looking for more mavericks who understand ideas. These people are worth their weight in gold.

Middle-managers didn't make great ideas people. Projects were cumbersome, took too long and cost too much. Market research became the costly corporate crutch that replaced decision making.

Top people didn't have time to mess about with variables. They wanted us to get on with it. But as soon as a brand development brief went down the organisational ladder, problems occurred. Most middle managers didn't have the muscle or the confidence to buy a single idea. They needed options. And they needed an outside authority – the market researcher – to buttress the decisions they took.

The base idea for Cîroc was to create the world's first grape vodka. It emerged as the first and only response to the brief – to create a brand with a compelling proposition versus Grey Goose. That process took less than a month.

But then the trouble started. The client's demand was for half a dozen alternatives, names, packages, concepts and 'mood boards. The whole process took about a year and cost close to a million dollars – to end up with that same grape vodka. I call that 'undue diligence'. Had we pitched that idea to people at the top of the organisation it would have been completed in a fraction of the time and for very little money.

"The harder I practise, the luckier I get." It took about 4 years to begin to understand what we were doing.

Gary Player, the golfer, said that. And he was right. It took several years of trial and error to 'get lucky'. The first work we did was highly speculative. We hid behind a barrage of ideas. We weren't confident about which would work. But also, I suspect, our clients weren't 100 per cent sure what they were expecting either.

You need mileage on the job to acquire self-assurance – and that applies to creators and buyers alike. Baileys happened after we'd been working with Tom Jago at IDV for four years. By then we were on the same wavelength. He was too grown up to want to mess about with multiple solutions.

We survived a long time working on minor projects for IDV – Green Island, Kenya Cane, Kenya Gold. I was even sent to New York to test three variants of a French wine brand name to settle an argument. Two days in Central Park with a tape recorder asking American passers-by to choose one from three obscure French words. Crazy. Well, it cost a fraction of the formal research estimate we received.

But despite this fallow period with nothing much to show for it, someone on high at IDV must have thought that we'd deliver in the end. I think perhaps we did.

A team of people with complementary skills is the best way to start out in brand innovation. But keep it small.

If a company were to ask me how to set up an innovation group, I'd say start with a team of two and work up. Slowly. And it doesn't matter how big the company might be.

I'd start with a marketing or advertising jack-of-all-trades, someone who is passionate, opinionated and hugely inquisitive. You know the type: they always have ideas for other people's brands. They are 'kibitzers' who interfere in all aspects of the business. And they are more likely to be marketing people. And they probably don't fit very well into an orthodox marketing framework.

That person should be good enough with words to write copy and should be capable of planning, running and reporting on focus groups.

The other half should be a technical generalist, a chemist or engineer who has a decent grasp of all aspects of development. The best people I met were able to broaden their knowledge by attending focus groups and I would have loved to see one of them run their own groups. Sadly that never happened.

It is good to have an operation where people have different skills. They can admire each other for their expertise rather than run into competition all the time.

Outside of those two, other services can be brought in as and when necessary. And the core couple can aim to build alliances with innovation enthusiasts in other departments as things progress.

When I left Diageo they had substantial innovation hubs in the UK, the US and the Far East employing vast numbers. I worked with these groups on occasion but cannot honestly say they were more successful than our small 'bucket shop' groups. Even modern brands Cîroc and Tanqueray Ten were created by small teams.

Marketing by mindset. Overpriced? Overkill? Overrated.

I always wondered about the technical wisdom of target grouping, especially in the new products field. On occasion there was a challenge to a new idea: "Yes, but, who exactly is our target group? What is their motivation?"

Back in the day it was simple. Targeting was coded by age – 18–24 for example – and something loosely described as socio-economic grouping – AB or C2DE. Crude tools but we knew we were after old or young, rich or poor, urban or rural.

Then it became more sophisticated. Or was it more convoluted? Targeting became psychographic: we would be required to create vodkas for hunter-gatherers or gins for late aspirers. The business had lapsed into gobbledygook.

I am not sure I believed in any of that stuff. We hadn't a clue who the Baileys target group would be. It was a novel idea which would find its audience. Stubbs, the Australian white rum (see page 194), was loosely aimed at men through its high strength and its macho heritage. And we arbitrarily decided that Aqua Libra should appeal to top fashion models, so we sold it in places where they might go. No psychographic credentials anywhere.

I always preferred what I termed the 'benefit out' approach. Smirnoff Black was conceived as 'the world's smoothest vodka'. That was its benefit. Shout it from the rooftops and it would find its target. I am not sure that 'marketing by mindset' would have been more effective.

In short, build a new brand on a compelling product story and broadcast that story as loudly as you can.

You need to buy services outside, but beware the paradigm-busting, out-of-the-box thinking charlatan.

It would be pointless and ridiculously expensive to have all the necessary skills and services in-house. You need to go outside for help and to widen your perspective.

I have witnessed any number of pan-global, paradigm-busting, outside-the-box charlatans in my time and in some cases worked in parallel with them on client developments. I can remember when we started out back in the seventies, a very dear friend who owned a large design consultancy gave me this advice: "Break your service down into as many individual components as you can. Then give each component a brand name. And then charge for each one". We never got around to doing it but so-called systematic innovation programmes abound and, from what I observed, they generated more invoices than ideas.

Innovation consultants and all who sail in them

Being a one-man band for much of my business life I was often up against the big battalions. I met people who specialised in 'breaking paradigms' or 'thinking outside the box'. Brand development can be a sexy business but it's also shrouded with uncertainty. There are a lot of snake oil practitioners out there peddling magic ideation formulas and infallible research techniques which are said to guarantee success – but at an enormous cost. This kind of hype can be very comforting to a diffident mid-level marketing manager who is desperate for reassurance as he or she leaps into the unknown. I am not sure that this kind of thing works anywhere near as well as my much simpler approach.

Design was a key part of what
we did. Over the years we developed
a modus operandi for getting the best
out of designers.

We discovered early in the piece that the best design came from
small companies, even solo operators. Howard Waller, Gordon
Smith, Bob Wagner et al were the people who physically did the
design. They were not supported by glib 'suits' who provided the
lavish foreplay that preceded design presentations. I can even
recall one company using a resting actor to do the introduction
to a design pitch. It was hugely entertaining but we didn't give
them the job.

   We developed a method of assessing design presentations which
worked pretty well on most of the work we did. It went like this:

 ✱ We generally invited companies to pitch who had some
    track record in alcoholic beverage design. And on that
    basis we asked them not to show us lengthy presentations
    of their past work.
 ✱ We asked designers not to do any speculative work but to
    come in and talk to a small team from our side about the brief.
    It was the quality of their thinking about our problem that
    would persuade us to give them the business.
 ✱ We also insisted that no more than two people should attend
    the meeting, one of whom should be the person who was
    directly responsible for the design. People like Howard Waller
    and Gordon Smith were more than capable of doing solo
    presentations, but other designers needed a bit of hand-
    holding to get their ideas across.

I continue to be amazed at the reverence with which market research is regarded. It is the creaky crutch on which marketing leans.

There is no such thing as the perfect idea. What we must hope for is the best possible idea in the minds of the creator and the buyer at the time that it is commissioned. This is probably the most important and most difficult concept that I have to communicate in this section of the book.

There is a comfort device in marketing that doesn't exist in any other branch of business. It's called market research. In the more conventional approach to brand development you get a brief, develop a range of ideas in response to the brief and then subject them to an intensive and expensive research programme to identify a winner. It's called 'listening to the consumer' and it's regarded as the professional way to do things. And sometimes it works. But often it doesn't.

But it can also help to 'dumb down' ideas. Consumers often don't know what they like – but they invariably like what they know. So they pull ideas back into familiar territory.

Having been involved with market research since 1960, I am aware that it's a pretty crude tool even now, 50 years on. It is generally held that 90 per cent of all new products fail. Yet in most cases large global corporations' new brand ideas are subjected to exhaustive research analysis. But what price a science that gets it wrong nine times out of ten?

In 1984 I wrote a piece in a UK marketing magazine in which I asked the question 'if nine out of ten heavily researched ideas fail how is it that we never blame research for these failures?' There are all kinds of excuses for failure but faulty research is never one of them. Guinness Light came out of research a sure-fire, copper-bottomed winner but it was a disaster. The little research we did on Baileys was pretty unenthusiastic so we made a judgement call and look what happened. Expecting a bombardment from the pillars of the research establishment, I sat back and waited. Nothing happened. Nobody said a word.

Can you imagine a CFO going to the board with half a dozen financial plans and then asking bankers and economists to pronounce on which is best? You can't. And the same applies to other branches of business. People are employed to be specialists: in finance, legal, sales and production. Shouldn't marketing people and brand development people be specialists too?

Research budgets are huge and yet in times of financial hardship they are invariably increased rather than reduced. I once made a presentation to the London office of a global detergents giant. To provoke discussion I said "why not put an embargo on all market research for the next two years? You would save about £20 million. (It was 30 years ago, so it would be much more now.) To replace it get your people to think more. And go back into the files and use the research you've already paid for".

I really believe this approach would pay off. There are very bright people out there who would respond brilliantly to doing their own thinking and making expert decisions. Just throw away the crutch and see what happens.

Here are a few ideas on how I think companies might conduct their research programmes. They will save time, a great deal of money and will engage their people more intimately with the products they make:

✱ **The research you've already done is an important company asset. Trouble is that in most cases when a study is completed it is consigned to oblivion.** I have already raised this issue above, but it's worth re-emphasising. The start point for every product development programme I worked on was a rummage through the company's existing data store. I was surprised at how quickly people in companies, often assisted by their consultants, rushed to commission new research. Markets don't change that quickly and information that was three, four or five years old always provided valuable insights to help solve new problems.

I wonder how many companies catalogue past research so that, at the press of a button, it is possible to determine that the expensive programme about to go into the field was actually carried out three or four years ago?

* Any intelligent person can carry out a focus group. I was transformed from a 'behind the mirror' observer to a research moderator in 24 hours. The person who had been commissioned to carry out some groups called in sick, the facility had been booked and the recruitment completed, so we would have wasted a lot of money if we'd cancelled the work. It was in New York. I volunteered to moderate. The research was on an idea that I had developed and I welcomed the opportunity for some eye contact with potential consumers. Having observed numerous groups in the past it was no big deal.

That was back in 1979 and since then I have carried out over 500 groups in the UK, US, Canada, Australia, South Africa, Ireland and India. And I developed methodology which was used in a number of non-English-speaking countries including Taiwan, Thailand, Korea, Germany, Japan, France, Spain, Poland and Russia. And almost all of this work was carried out to evaluate ideas that I had produced.

This transformation to becoming a group moderator was no huge achievement. Running a focus group is like running a meeting. The longer you can keep your own mouth shut, the better. It's about being able to listen.

* I would have company marketing and technical people running their own focus groups. In most cases, groups are attended by crowds of marketing and advertising people – even research managers and planners. Why don't they do the groups? Think of the money you'd save. It is a real help in a development to

THE JACK NAPIER COMPANY

CANADIAN WHISKY FOR THE CONNOISSEUR

THE JACK NAPIER COMPANY has been established to unearth some of Canada's hidden assets. We have combed the country looking for the most interesting and unusual whiskies and we proudly offer them to discerning drinkers. Some are only available in limited quantity.

OUR LIST

SINGLE BARREL is unusual in that the blend of Rye Malt and Fine Grain whiskies have been married together from the start of their distillation. (Most whiskies are aged separately and then married just before they are bottled.) This whisky matures just like a fine wine and has a great smoothness and elegance.

Our MALTED RYE can be described as the Canadian equivalent of a Scottish Single Malt. Made only from Malted Rye Whisky from a single distillery, it is a truly 'big' whisky full of oaky flavour and character. It is a whisky that takes time to learn, but the experience is well worth it.

DOUBLE WOOD is a blend of Rye and Grain Whiskies which is aged first in old oak barrels and later in Spanish sherry wood. The result is a whisky of wonderful complexity: woody and almost earthy on the nose, with a soft, mellow style to the finish. The sherry wood gives it its deep, rich colour.

Most distilleries set aside a small quantity of their very best whisky to enhance the quality of their younger whiskies when they are blended.

Our DISTILLER'S RESERVE is a 15 year old whisky with all the character that ageing brings and a milky smoothness of finish. It is only available in limited quantities.

STRAIGHT RYE is an aged blend of Rye Whiskies with no Grains added. Aged Rye is unusual in that maturation not only smoothes and softens the taste but it also increases the body of the whisky. The result is a whisky of unusual 'boldness', almost succulent in taste. It is a truly unusual example of the distiller's art.

JACK NAPIER & COMPANY, SWEETWATER, ALBERTA

confront the consumer face-to-face rather than hiding behind a one-way mirror. You can follow your instincts rather than stick rigidly to a script.

People have suggested on occasion that researching your own ideas can represent a compromise of objectivity. I don't think that ever happened in my case. And anyway, to develop powerful ideas you need to be subjective.

✱ Get consumers to rate real brands not hypothetical concepts. One of the first principles I established about research was that you should always introduce a new idea to the consumer as one that is already on the market, that is real. We are the experts. We want people to see the idea as a fait accompli not some hypothetical concept, open to modification. Consumers love playing amateur designer and we don't want that.

In some cases we would have finished packs and products. But if we didn't, we developed a very inexpensive and effective way of presenting new ideas as if they existed. This involved writing a magazine article describing the brand clearly and objectively. (Editorial copy has more credibility than does an advertisement.) The Coole Swan piece presented as Rainbow (see page 321) was based on an authentic magazine format and was supported by a computer-generated bottle and a product for tasting.

But you don't always have to go that far. The Jack Napier example opposite was presented as a company brand catalogue featuring a range of Canadian Whiskies which we wanted to evaluate before going to the expense of commissioning package design. Once you are clear about an idea, you can produce material very quickly and at virtually no cost.

The key principle is that you should develop your idea completely before testing it. Take decisions on price and product and make a full proposition to the consumer. Don't let respondents play 'mix and match' with ideas. You will invariably end up in the middle with the least challenging outcome.

This technique is not confined to drinks. We used it on everything from real estate to olive oil margarine. And the magazine article device also works very well in presenting ideas to clients.

✻ Keeping consumers honest. Attending focus groups in the early seventies, I noticed that ideas were presented for discussion in open forum. An idea was shown and there followed a free-for-all where the most assertive individual dominated discussion and influenced everyone else's opinions. It still happens.

To counter this, I developed an extremely simple method. First, circulate an assessment form where respondents put their name, their views on the item shown, and a rating out of ten to indicate interest in buying the product. People fill out the form without discussion and, on completion, they are de-briefed individually within the group. This way we get 'uninfected' responses and the rating ensures that respondents are held to their original opinions. Open debate only takes place after these individual opinions have been expressed.

The beauty of this system is that you get both positive and negative feedback in the same group. In research for the brand St Leger, only one woman in one group wrote down that she didn't like the name 'Prost' (see page 229). So we changed it. Groups aren't about consensus. They are forums for learning about your ideas. A single response, positive or negative, can be a jewel.

And the other real benefit of this method is that it makes groups really easy to follow for the moderator and the people behind the one-way mirror.

Name : *Jane Doe*

Group No : 4

You will be shown an article from a magazine describing a new drink you may not have tried before. Please read it carefully and write down your comments on the drink: what do you think it might taste like, how does it appeal to you and do you have any particular likes or dislikes about the drink? Then please rate it on a 0-10 scale to indicate your interest in buying it in a bar, restaurant or liquor store. (0 means 'not at all interested', 5 means 'undecided', 10 means 'extremely interested' and so on.)

A bit annoyed at the by-line on what is obviously a paragraph of ad copy and 'my drink to watch' is patronising. However, playing up the 'lower sweetness' and 'organic cocoa and vanilla' is a smart move. Sounds like a more complex and grown up version of Baileys. I'd definitely keep an eye out for it. Matte bottle and elegant font adds to the sense of a drink for adult women rather than teenagers. Daft name though. 8/10

NEWSPAPER

FOOD

What's New?

RAINBOW
Double Dairy
CREAM LIQUEUR

SINGLE MALT · DOUBLE CREAM

DRINK WATCH

By Kim Corbett

My drink to watch is RAINBOW CREAM from County Cork in Ireland. Made from Double Cream and Single Malt Irish Whiskey, it's exceptionally smooth and its lower sweetness means you really can taste the organic vanilla and cocoa in the blend. It's a real change from sugary-sweet mainstream products. RAINBOW is the first cream to get out of BAILEYS' shadow and at £18.99 occupies a new top-shelf position in the category. And I love the white frosted bottle.

One brief. One solution. Tough Sale.

In the 1960s, while plodding my way as an account manager in conservative London advertising agencies, I cast an envious eye at creative 'hot shop' Collett Dickenson Pearce (CDP). Legend had it that they only ever produced a single campaign solution to a client brief. "How could they do that?" I thought. The culture then was to hedge your bets. You would go to clients with a number of advertising solutions and let them make the call.

Then Baileys happened. Baileys Irish Cream.

Baileys was (coincidentally) developed CDP style. We went to Dublin with one idea, a cream liqueur or nothing: one brand name, one package design, one product.

The Irish company bought it and it worked.

I could see what CDP meant. There is no such thing as a perfect idea. But if you put all your skill and passion and commitment into finding the best solution you can, you are more likely to come up with a great one. And it helps if you have a client who is on the same wavelength and also sees it as the answer to his problem.

Every successful brand after Baileys was created on the same principle. One idea. Le Piat d'Or, Aqua Libra, Purdey's, Sheridan's, J&B Jet, Spey Royal, The Singleton, Smirnoff Black, Tanqueray Ten, Coole Swan and Cîroc (well, almost). If there were any issues, they were ironed out in conversation or a couple of focus groups.

I fell foul of a number of professional marketing people who said "How can you present just one idea?" My response was "How can you not?"

It is actually very easy to come up with multi-solutions to a brief. If you do this sort of thing as your day job, you can churn out half a dozen plausible ideas in a couple of hours. Then you put them all into an expensive popularity contest.

As I said earlier, the lower down the management scale you go the harder it is to sell a single idea. At this level people are often reluctant to apply any filters at all to a slick, bulked-up new brand presentation. I have seen some truly terrible ideas find their way into costly research programmes because no one had the courage to dump them. 'Let the consumer decide' is the comfortable cop-out.

As the world became more risk-averse the demand was for multiple answers. Give us options, let us see variety - and then pass the buck to the consumer. Market research would be the final arbiter. But, as I hope I have shown in this book, that's a cop out. This approach doesn't work.

I think you can only really appreciate the value of a single solution if you've tried to create ideas yourself. And if you have a client who has shared some of the agony with you, that really helps. He or she will know what you are both looking for – and recognise it when it emerges.

The game of the name can be one of the most exasperating aspects of brand development.

Coming up with names for new brands was a tough task. Getting people to agree to them could be a nightmare. It could take weeks, even months, to find the perfect name and all it took to demolish it was someone saying "well, it does nothing for me".

Names are also hard to sell. Very occasionally you get lucky and a name sells itself. Aqua Libra was an instant hit.

Back in my Kerrygold days, before I got into brand development, the client, Tony O'Reilly, suggested that Irish surnames might sound 'stagey' and not be taken seriously. Hoolihans, or indeed O'Reillys Irish Butter, was not what he was after, so we created Kerrygold.

That led us to Baileys, a more serious Anglo-Irish name. I was amazed that it passed without debate. And by the time we got to Dublin, it was bolstered by the support of a finished label and a fully-dressed bottle. It looked totally convincing.

A useful lesson I learned concerned naming extensions of existing brands. A new variant should always compel the use of the core brand in a bar 'call'. Ask for Tanqueray Ten, not Ten alone. And Baileys 'The Whiskey' was joined at the hip to its parent brand.

Smirnoff Black began with no sub-name at all, encouraging buyers to create their own 'call'.

But it was later dumbed down through inserting 'Black' on the label. No art there.

Companies can be quite pusillanimous about brand names, looking to make them idiot-proof. But people are more intelligent and savvy than we think and can handle complex foreign names. Look at English football teams nowadays.

What kind of better mousetrap do you want? One that kills more mice or one that makes you look good?

Functional or emotional benefits? Which is your preference? My choice is functional, a 'sale in the mouth' over a 'sale in the mind'. Smirnoff Black is a palpably smoother vodka; Tanqueray Ten is a fresher, cleaner-tasting gin: Coole Swan is perceptibly less sweet than Baileys and has a discernible whiskey after-taste. All those brands had a tale to tell and a claim to make. And those claims were engineered. We were looking to create better products. I always had tough retailers like Max the Hat in my head when I started on a brand journey. 'What's so special about your brand, buddy boy? Give me the facts.' I needed an answer to that kind of question.

I cut my business teeth in the 1960s on clients like Procter & Gamble, and was influenced by Rosser Reeves and his USP idea. I have always looked for functional reasons to differentiate my brands from their competitors. Even back then, Kerrygold had a 'pint of cream in every packet'. To me the better mousetrap is about eliminating more mice, quickly and efficiently. Making you, the user, look like a caring, hygienic homemaker is of secondary concern.

But functional benefits aren't considered sexy. The processes of finding a proposition which focuses on how a buyer looks and feels – the emotional benefit – seems now to be the modern way. But consider this: it is a lot more expensive communicating an emotional story than selling a factual advantage. I could never understand why Smirnoff doesn't make more of its amazing smooth taste, or why Tanqueray Ten barely makes reference to its uniquely fresh gin flavour and its fresh botanicals.

I think emotional benefits are a lot easier to create than a genuine, perceptible difference between one vodka product and another. That's why they are preferred by advertising and marketing people. But most emotional propositions are pretty ordinary.

Smirnoff Black illustrates this point. At the time it was created, Smirnoff was down in the dumps with about as much prestige as own-label vodka. But as soon as we came up with a product which actually tasted better, tough-minded New York Absolut and Stoli drinkers were offering to switch.

"But it's only from Smirnoff" I said, "Why would you buy it instead of Absolut?" "Because it tastes better, it's smoother" was the response. And even when I suggested that other groups I'd researched didn't rate it (not true), they stuck to their guns. I don't think I ever saw an ad for 'Smooth Smirnoff'. It's not too late.

And sometimes being better could mean being different. Aqua Libra was a product that polarised opinion. Some people hated it, but a significant number of people adored it. And that was good enough for us. If I were developing a brand to compete with Coke, for example, I would look for 5 per cent of their users who might be persuaded to switch. But can traditional research and marketing cope with such a small number? Somehow I don't think so.

We always tried to live with our products.

Another simple idea we employed was to live with our products. There can be a tendency to hold products at arm's length in our science-obsessed marketing environment. We wait for research reports to tell us whether a product is acceptable and we can create an intellectual distance between ourselves, our products and their consumers.

This applies particularly in food and drink products. I can recall a meeting many years ago at Birds Eye. A new fish product was presented to the chairman with glittering research results. He turned to the assembled group and said "We're not doing it. I don't like it. It tastes awful". He was a product-obsessive. And he was right.

We took a case of St Leger (orange juice, white wine and mineral water) to Miami. We were on another job which involved working at night so we played tennis during the day. We tasted the drink after a couple of sets in blistering heat. It just wasn't sweet enough. So Mac Macpherson called the UK and asked them to up the sweetness.

With Coole Swan we had 231 goes at getting it right. Our own sampling told us not to make it as sweet as other cream liqueurs – and to make it taste like a quality whiskey-based drink. We were creating a premium alcoholic beverage, not a dessert.

Tom Peters, excellence
and the IDV way.

In 1982 Tony Carey, a client from Ireland, gave me a book that had
become an overnight bestseller in the US. It was called *In Search of
Excellence* and was written by Robert H Waterman and Tom Peters.
It was a great read and what it said was that the procedures and
practices that gave rise to brands like Baileys and Le Piat d'Or were
OK. Intuition and speculation could fuel innovation at the expense of
excessive analysis.

I gave a copy to Tom Jago who read it and then ordered a dozen
copies and circulated them to members of the IDV board. This had
a significant influence on the progress of brand development in IDV
in the years to come.

The breakfast of champions

Perhaps the most notable idea taken from the 'Excellence' book
was the idea of 'Brand Champions'. In the book it said that to
plough their way through a conservative corporate environment,
brands needed to have champions. These were bloody-minded
individualists who wouldn't take no for an answer if they thought
they had a good idea on their hands.

IDV was full of people like that, so championship became part
of the management landscape. Anyone at a certain level could
summon someone from the brand development team and
requisition and sponsor a new brand. I can remember David Defty,
the finance director, becoming heavily involved with a project he
initiated. He would attend focus groups and design meetings and
got closer to the viscera of a brand than he would ever have done
from his ivory tower without this champion's culture.

And the idea wasn't just a local one, IDV companies abroad were also encouraged to adopt 'championship' and I can recall travelling as far afield as Brazil to create a brand for their CEO, Hermann Schmalzigaug. The brand was a cachaça called Berro d'Agua but, being the late 1980s, it may have been ahead of its time.

The system was a real boost to the overall creativity of the organisation and worked through the eighties and early nineties. It 'petered out' as IDV took over Heublein, merged with Guinness United Distillers and Tim Ambler left to become a professor of marketing at London Business School. New cultures were being adopted and absorbed. But many of the best brands developed in that period were champion driven.

Central funding made the world go round

One of the other important components in the IDV way was the availability of a cache of money to fund development anywhere within the organisation. A small outpost of the organisation, Gilbeys Canada, came up with an inspired idea which Tim Ambler coined a 'me-one'. The Canadians had observed the explosive growth of De Kuyper's Peachtree Schnapps in the US and decided to create a similar brand for sale in other markets. They would make hay elsewhere while De Kuyper soldiered on building its brand in the US.

The brand, Archers, became a success in a number of IDV markets and pre-empted the global growth of Peachtree. IDV made funding available for the Canadians and gave them access to any central services they required. It now became possible for any company in the network to enter the brand development pool. They could become brand champions in their own right.

SO THAT'S THE END of my story. I think the quote opposite by Tom Peters admirably sums up what I've been trying to get across in this book.

" Life is pretty simple: you do some stuff. Most fails. Some works. You do more of what works. If it works big others quickly copy it. Then you do something else. The trick is the doing something else. "

Used by permission of Tom Peters.
See **tompeters.com** for more of his work

Thanks

As I hope I have explained throughout this book, creating new brands was a team game. I would put an idea on the table and designers and product people would bring it to life. After that, marketing and commercial people would make it happen. I owe them all my gratitude.

Hugh Seymour-Davies for putting up with me for so long and remaining a perfect gentleman.

Tom Jago who opened the door to the wonderful world of wine and spirits.

Mac Macpherson, sadly now departed, partnered me through a golden era at IDV and was as much a friend as a client. He enjoyed reading an early draft of this book.

Tim Ambler for his inspiration when we worked together and his kind offer to write a foreword for this book.

Barbara Bryant who tolerated a curmudgeonly first-time author for so many years and provided her intelligence and analytical skill in helping me to finalise the book.

The designers for transforming my flights of imagination into objects of beauty and commercial success: the late Howard Waller, Gerry Barney, Bob Wagner, Kit Cooper, Darrell Ireland and Gordon Smith.

I read Andrew Cracknell's *The Real Mad Men*, designed by Simon Daley, and had to have Simon design my book. His skill is here for all to see and his knowledge and experience in the publishing business has been of immense help in steering me through.

I was looking for a cover designer who would live up to the standards set by Waller, Wagner et al. I found Jamie Keenan. He offered me one idea. It was brilliant. And I bought it.

My thanks to Salima Hirani for her meticulous fine-tuning of my manuscript. It was a pleasure working with her.

The late David Dand, the true champion of Baileys, the brand that started it all.

The late Donal Cruise O'Brien who spent so much time persuading me that I could and should write a book.

David Phelan and Adrian Walker were my partners in Coole Swan, a fabulous brand of our own.

James Maw shook the dust off my early draft and helped me bring it back to life. I was deeply grateful for his kindness and commitment.

Catherine Buchanan-Richardson for her encouragement and enthusiasm for this venture.

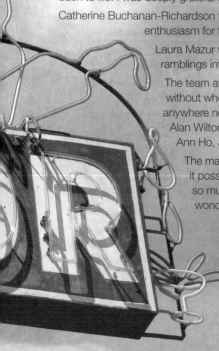

Laura Mazur who transformed my undisciplined ramblings into the coherent whole that is this book.

The team at IDV/Diageo technical innovation without whom none of these ideas would have been anywhere near as good as they eventually became: Alan Wilton, Colin Purdey, Steve Wilson, Chris Armes, Ann Ho, Jim Milne, Jim Beveridge, and many others.

The management of IDV and Diageo for making it possible for me to operate for so long, see so much of the world and create so many wonderful brands on their behalf.

Index